PORTRAIT OF

A GHETTO SCHOOL

PORTRAIT OF
A GHETTO SCHOOL

ADDIE D. JONES

VANTAGE PRESS

New York   Washington   Hollywood

FIRST EDITION

Copyright © 1973 by Addie D. Jones

Published by Vantage Press, Inc.
516 West 34th Street, New York, N.Y. 10001

Manufactured in the United States of America

Standard Book No. 533-00631-7

IN MEMORY OF MY BELOVED
HUSBAND,

C. S. JONES

FOREWORD

It has been said that our youth, in any age, are our most precious asset and their training is our most important business.

I believe that too much of the education and training of our young people has been left to the schools. The efforts of schools must be supported and complemented by other agencies and institutions in our society.

Problems that confront our educational institutions are many. For one thing, Americans have not been sufficiently of one mind as to what they want the schools to do, and the educators themselves have been unsure as to how best to do the job.

Americans generally have been unwilling to provide the money that education needs. Another important problem has been the inequality of educational opportunity afforded some Americans because they happened to be members of a minority group insofar as geography, race, or economic and social conditions are concerned.

But schools have wrought well despite handicaps. This has been particularly true where black schools are concerned. Any evaluation of the progress that has been made must take this into account.

Portrait of a Ghetto School is such an account. It is a story of one school, but is typical of many. It tells the story of how a community at the turn of the century, with an abiding faith in the efficacy of education, came together to literally build a school. It is a story of undaunted leaders in the community, of selfless, able, and committed teachers, of successive generations of students who believed that education was the vital margin in the development of a community, of a people, of a society.

It is a belief and a faith that could not have been expressed better than was done by that great American statesman, former President Lyndon Baines Johnson, when he said: "Education is mankind's only hope. Education is the imperative of a universal and lasting peace. . . . Education is the key that unlocks progress in the struggle against hunger and want and injustice wherever they may exist on earth. It is the path which now beckons us toward the planets and the stars. Above all else, it is the well-spring of freedom and peace."

Portrait of a Ghetto School concerns itself with a school that has through the years tried to keep abreast, has grown, developed, and improved to meet the demands, challenges, and needs of the times.

It is a portrait of a school that is proud of its tradition and its on-going program; a school that has taken the so-called disadvantaged and shown that they could measure up to the best in the land; a school that is proud of the accomplishments of its graduates, many of whom have gone on to colleges, universities, and into the various walks of life and are making outstanding contributions.

The author is unquestionably qualified to write this story. Mrs. Addie D. Jones has been a vital part of this school for nearly half a century. She has made contributions which few, anywhere, in any school, can match. Many, many of the young people of whom the school is proud came under her influence as teacher and later as guidance counselor. She was a part of the history of which she has written. She helped greatly in making this history.

Louis B. Hobson
January 1972

INTRODUCTION

A ghetto school that produced men and women of distinction, and what made it tick is the major concern of this dissertation. In taking a look at the background of this school, the narrative would go like this: The idea was initiated and the school was organized by blacks for blacks around the close of the 19th century when slavery and emancipation were fresh in the minds of Negroes. As is quite well known, this was a time when there were few opportunities for black people in any endeavor, and education was, perhaps, at the bottom of the totem pole.

This narrative underscores many of the difficulties and hardships encountered in building an institution to serve the ever increasing black population rapidly growing in this mid-south suburban area. It aims to point up the vision and foresight of the founders and the spirit that motivated an underprivileged people striving to lessen the burden of poverty, want, and ignorance.

Furthermore, this sketch is aimed to show the difficulties encountered by these founders to keep their objectives alive and to pass them on to generations who were to follow.

The kinds of students this school had to serve are an important part of this treatise. It will be noted that many changes were made, from small homeowners to renters and, in many cases, highly transit families. Consequently the types of students were changing from time to time. It seems as if by some power of fate, or by man's design, each administration has been fully aware of the years of sacrifice and hardships of the founders and has perpetuated the spirit behind the endeavor.

Not only is this essay written to preserve the memory of the work of black men near the close of the 19th century, but it aims to encourage, inspire, and motivate the young blacks of today who have misgivings about the possibilities of achievement in the presence of difficult odds and what makes for a good life.

A major portion of this history brings into focus some of the many young blacks who lived with the spirit of the founders, administrators, and teachers at Manassas School and found in them the types of inspiring and motivating forces that became an important part of their lives. As a result, they went out with a determination to become a viable entity in the mainstream of American life. Thus they journeyed from ghetto school to success—accomplishments and developments which permitted them an opportunity for tremendous service and personal achievement.

Important too, I think that a description of the community is of great value in assessing the growth of the school. The setting of this endeavor was in a little community where businessmen felt the urge to locate factories and lumber mills and other kinds of industries. These businesses furnished jobs for both laboring blacks and whites, who were dependent on weekly take-home pay for their living needs. This sparsely populated area, clearly outside of the city limits at that time but close enough to accommodate those who were inclined to make the trip to the outlying car stops or use the horse and buggy, meant the difference between urban shopping or bartering at a country grocery store.

But long before factories were moved into this section there were blacks occupying the muddy roads and soggy fields, extracting what they could from the available land.

The blacks in this neighborhood had no school nearby. They were forced to walk several miles to the nearest school which carried them as high as the eighth grade, consequently only few were able to get even a beginner's education, so it was the founders who knew and who cared. Somebody had to care enough to try.

Finally included in this script are many and varied methods instituted by the administrators in their quest for approaches to educate, compensate, and motivate discouraged and frustrated children. The ingenuity of the administrators has been emphasized here because it was without a doubt that their dedicated conviction and work resulted in the perpetuation of this great institution with its outstanding heritage and admirable accomplishments.

CONTENTS

PORTRAIT OF

A GHETTO SCHOOL

SOMEBODY HAD TO CARE ENOUGH TO TRY

According to older citizens of that North Memphis community, Spencer Johnson, then living across the street from a huge vacant field known as Driving Park, had this strong feeling about the future of the Negro: He advanced

Spencer Johnson

17

the theory that the Negro must move into the mainstream of life in America through education and constructive thinking if he would live successfully and work in this fast-moving civilization beside his white counterpart.

It is evident that Spencer Johnson could foresee that for the black man to survive in a state of decency and respect he must be trained to fit into the many and varied aspects of the world of work. It is also evident that he could understand the great potential present among those who were not generally thought of as being capable of absorbing scholarly concepts.

So Mr. Johnson gathered around him his best friends and supporters and sold them this idea. And they started something. They had to care enough to try. Any history of this movement would be incomplete and inaccurate without an introduction to the spirit of these immortal founders. They were men of vision, foresight, and dedication to the welfare of the race.

Attorney W. L. Terry, who lived until the early 1950s, and had been a member of the County Board of Education in 1900, wrote the following statement regarding the beginning of the school:

In the early history of this school and the neighborhood there was a man by the name of Spencer Johnson who took the lead in all the affairs, and who advocated the consolidation of the two small neighborhood schools into a school which was located in 1899 or 1900 on Manassas Street. He induced the former Board of Education, which was composed of Mr. Turner Buford and two other gentlemen, probably a Mr. Prescott and Mr. Judd, to place the school at that point in the midst of a growing Negro community.

To accomplish this task, Spencer Johnson solicited the interest and cooperation of J. A. Phillips, J. Harper, Godfrey Hack, W. F. Finney, Rev. Wm. H. Young, a Mr. Dunnaway, and C. McCombs. These men served as the

nucleus of an undertaking that was to prove of far-reaching effect to the Manassas community. These, and others with them, were also instrumental later on in petitioning the Board of Education for an eight-month term. When I came on the Board, I soon ascertained that he (Spencer Johnson) was a substantial citizen, worthy of confidence of the Board, and he worked continuously in the interest of the school, and took the forefront and the brunt of all work that was incident to the development of the school.

When the Board had funds for only six months of school, he would interest the neighbors in contributing to the fund to pay teachers so that an eight-month term would be given.

In all local affairs incident to the school neighborhood, we confided to Spencer Johnson, and he carried the same through the Board.

Of course Spencer had to be active in local welfare, community uplift, and civic matters of the 15th District in order to have the great influence carried by him in the section. He was right always, honest and progressive.

As stated above, it was the work of Spencer Johnson that established the Manassas Street School, and it was also his pleasure and duty to carry on all matters of business with the development of the school in the earlier stages which rested on his shoulders through 1914. (Signed) W. L. Terry, Attorney at Law.

Two members of the Manassas faculty, in 1952-53, did some research into the historical background of Manassas School. They were the late Mr. E. A. Teague, and the late Mrs. Willie Alma McWilliams-Walker, who sought this information for the fifty-third anniversary of the school. Mr. Teague was the assistant principal, and Mrs. Walker, a graduate of 1927, had been a teacher there after her high school graduation until her death. At the time they reported their information as having been obtained from the late Mr. R. E. Johnson, and his sister, the late Miss Evelyn Johnson,

Picture of Manassas School

son and daughter of the founder, Mr. Spencer Johnson. The foregoing information, contributed by Attorney W. L. Terry, was part of their quest for the actual background of the school.

Further information as to the early history of the school has been supplied by me through personal interviews with Mrs. Mable Williams Hughes (recently deceased) and two members of the Phillips family—Mrs. Effie Phillips Young, and her brother, Mr. Arthur Phillips. When the school was established, the Phillips' residence was located on Manassas Street, first house from the belt-line railroad. Both Mrs. Young and her brother, Arthur Phillips, are still living. They were among the first students who had attended the little two-room school when it opened in 1900.

Mrs. Young and Mr. Phillips informed me that the school was in a two-room frame structure, on the west side of Manassas Street north of the belt line, and they said that William H. Foote (deceased) was placed in charge of the school as principal.

Continuing the interview, they said that "by 1902 two more rooms had been added to the frame building, and the late Mrs. Laura Johnson Byas (daughter of Spencer Johnson) was employed as a teacher."

In 1904 the school was enlarged a second time. It was during this year that William H. Foote resigned in order to accept a letter-carrier position with the post office department, during which time he studied to complete the law course he began while serving as the first principal of Manassas School. Mr. Foote was succeeded by Miss Rose Washington, who later became his wife.

Mrs. Rose Washington Foote

Mrs. Rose Washington Foote served from 1904 to 1909. After the administration of Mrs. Foote, the school was placed in charge of Mrs. Cora P. Taylor.

Mrs. Cora P. Taylor

THE ADMINISTRATION OF MRS. CORA P. TAYLOR

It was during that year (1909) that the late Mrs. Mable Williams Hughes was appointed superintendent of the Shelby County schools. In the words of Mrs. Hughes during a personal interview in 1966: "I set out to find someone who could enter into the spirit of a growing community, someone who would sympathize with an underprivileged people."

Knowing something of the work of Mrs. Cora P. Taylor, who at the time was a teacher at Spring Hill County School at Raleigh, Tennessee, Mrs. Hughes appointed Mrs. Taylor as principal of Manassas School.

Continuing the personal interview with Mrs. Hughes, I was

asked to quote her as saying: "I can't say too much about Cora Taylor as a good teacher and principal. Her school was clean, and her students were neat and well behaved. They used to sing for me, and one day I had to leave the room. They sang like angels. The sweetest music I ever heard.

"There were no bad ones there, there were just those who were not so well prepared.

"There was no Negro high school in the county at that time. The schools were not adequate. But as money came along, some of it was used in the Negro School, and some in the white."

Mrs. Hughes served as superintendent until 1915. Meantime, Mrs. Cora Taylor had gone about among the people of the neighborhood to raise funds to relieve the crowded inconvenient situation which had arisen.

Along with the late Rev. L. A. Kemp, pastor of the neighborhood Baptist Church, and other leaders in the community, Mrs. Taylor was able to purchase a tract of land across the street from the school. This land was deeded to the County Board of Education, and, by 1915, when Miss Charl Williams, sister of Mrs. Mable Williams Hughes (who had resigned and married) became superintendent, the land was ready for school construction.

In 1918, the Board of Education erected a sixteen-room stucco building. For a short time only, Manassas School could accommodate her students. But the program of expansion was well under way.

According to Mrs. Hughes, Superintendent Charl Williams held all her meetings for Negro teachers in the stucco building. She scheduled institutes for training teachers in domestic science and art. Sewing machines and much other equipment were added.

Because of overcrowded conditions again in 1921, Mrs. Taylor again went to friends and patrons for financial solicitations. With student labor, and help from men in the neighborhood, there was erected a two-story frame building which served to house the industrial departments of the school. Meantime, the 9th grade was added, and the school was then geared toward the goal of a four-year high school.

Mrs. Hughes continued: "Miss Charl Williams, then superintendent, took a great deal of pride in the school. And when she had the opportunity she carried visitors out to see Manassas."

During this period, the County Board of Education used its influence to obtain Rosenwald support for Manassas School. Much was done by this funding toward the furnishing of additional equipment and teachers. Additions were made, such as library and librarian, chemistry and physics laboratories, and more machines for home economics department. By 1924, Manassas was rated as the largest Rosenwald School in the world.

A banner year in the history of this school was 1924, when Manassas had its first high-school graduating class, consisting of twelve students. Manassas was then one of the only two four-year high schools for Negroes in Shelby County.

By the time of the first graduation, Miss Charl Williams had resigned to become Secretary of Extension for the National Education Association, Washington, D.C. Miss Sue M. Powers succeeded Miss Williams, and is reported to have demonstrated equal interest and enthusiasm for the program at Manassas.

Mrs. Taylor's administration at Manassas School was marked by initiative, profound planning, and an indomitable will to make her educational program succeed. With this determination as her motivation, she worked doggedly at every endeavor.

Competitive sports was ushered into the school's program, among other things, as a by-product. Baseball, basketball, and football had become a feature of the secondary school program by the 1924-25 school year. One after the other, the teams were climbing to victorious feats. On one occasion when the players had no more secondary school teams to beat in West Tennessee, they challenged the Tennessee State

College team and covered themselves with glory for a brilliant performance.

In 1927, through the strenuous efforts and hard work of Mrs. Taylor—who personally hauled bricks from Millington by truck—a beige brick auditorium was erected on the campus by the patrons of the community.

The auditorium, still in use, has a seating capacity of 1,200. During the early years, the Gospel Temple Baptist Church had been used for all public affairs, concerts, and assemblies held by the school.

It is most difficult to assess the kind of spirit that permeated the lives of the graduates, the students, and the teachers of Manassas School in those days. The spirit was so high that it inspired the music teacher—at that time, Mrs. Georgia Quinn—to write the lyrics to a school song the title of which is "We'll Never Let Manassas Fall," and many generations have been inspired by these moving lines:

Gold and Blue, the emblem of Manassas,
Best old school of peace and unity,
Best old school there is in all creation,
The gold and blue, the sign of purity.

Gold and blue, it stands for peace and beauty,
Each Brave heart will answer to her call;
Hand in hand we stand to do our duty,
And we'll never let Manassas fall!

Chorus:

We'll never let Manassas fall,
For we love her the best of all.
We don't want to fight to show our might,
But when we start,
We'll fight, fight, fight!

In peace or war our voices ring,
And, oh, Manassas, we will sing.
At the sound of the call
We'll show them all,
We'll never let Manassas fall.

Mrs. Georgia P. Quinn

Late in 1927, Mrs. Taylor became seriously ill. And though no longer able to function as principal, she lived long enough to witness the transition of Manassas School into the city system by annexation of the district. Mrs. Taylor died in 1932, and her body was brought into the school building to be viewed by those who had known and loved her. The eulogy was said in the auditorium which now bears her name—The Cora P. Taylor Auditorium. A bronze bust of Mrs. Taylor has been placed above the auditorium entrance to commemorate her long years of service. Her great contribution still lives. Her name is a legend.

THE ADMINISTRATION OF J. ASHTON HAYES

The late Mr. J. Ashton Hayes was appointed principal of Manassas High School in 1929, during the illness of Mrs. Taylor.

His administration began just at a time when the Great Depression had retarded the physical growth of the plant. The school population had multiplied. The enrollment had reached 2,700, and facilities became much overcrowded. But nothing could be done until, under the National Recovery Act, a new fifty-room structure was attached to the auditorium and the old stucco building was razed. This improvement was made under the direction of the City Board of Education, with Mr. E. C. Ball serving as superintendent. The entire area surrounding Manassas School was annexed in 1930.

When Mr. Hayes walked into the situation as principal of Manassas School, his whole being was absorbed by a spirit as contagious as the most communicable of diseases. And under him the aspiration, determination, and the will to succeed seemed to take on new proportions.

As did his predecessors, Mr. Hayes fought long and hard for more and more improvements. He met a situation of overcrowded conditions, but many students seemed eager to prepare themselves for future service and decent living. It was not a great task for him to understand the spirit that motivated these young people because, far and near, the work of Manassas School was on the lips of all who had shared both in its spirit and in its growth.

Expansion and growth was the theme song early in his administration. But the country had just been caught in the grip of one of the greatest depressions of the century. During the administration of Franklin Delano Roosevelt, Manassas

Mr. J. Ashton Hayes and wife Rosalind

School was one of the first in this section to benefit from the National Recovery Act program.

After a quarter of a century of service, Mr. Hayes retired in 1953. He had been a stern taskmaster. He had preserved many of the traditions that had been established by the former administrator, Mrs. Cora P. Taylor, most spectacular of which was the silence bell. For the beginning of the school-day, or the reconvening of school from recess, the first bell that rang meant complete silence; not a whisper or the sound of a step could be heard until a second sounding of the bell. At this time the students were conditioned to walk calmly to their places and begin work.

28

At the end of this quarter of a century with Mr. J. Ashton Hayes at the helm, many displayed their passionate love for him in various ways. He was a symbol of stability for the school in the northern section of Memphis which they loved so deeply. The honors ceremony brought tears and laughter, joy and sorrow.

A part of the narration at that ceremony may give the reader some impression as to the actual character of this man. It may also reveal some of the kinds of problems encountered in this school and neighborhood.

The faculty and new principal planned a night to honor Mr. Hayes and to say their fond good-bye. It was done by a narrator, who wrote the following lines that were directed to him. The title was:

THROUGH THE YEARS WITH J. ASHTON HAYES
By Mrs. Addie D. Jones

It went thusly:

You came to Memphis in the prime of your life with a good basic foundation in education, seasoned with a reasonable portion of experience, and a wealth of good common sense. You looked vigorous, ruddy, and robust, so that the coloring beneath your skin rose to the surface upon the least provocation giving the appearance of one fit for any eventuality. It was nothing unusual to see you engaged in a game of baseball with the boys.

Your footsteps were sturdy and swift, giving your body a quick movement representing an active and perhaps an apprehensive mind. I have not been able to ascertain what was in your pockets. All I could see of your personal wealth was a well used postdated automobile, some well fitted, carefully selected attire, some brightly shined shoes which always pointed their toes toward each other, and a change in necktie for each well pressed suit.

Your mellow wit and delightful sense of humor

combined to offset that growling, commanding voice that sent a chill-like shiver up from the knees of those who did not know you too well. But it wasn't too long before it was generally known that your "bark was worse than your bite."

It was also soon discerned that beneath the ruggedness of the physical body, aside from that growl in the voice and apart from the hard swollen hands, which you referred to as "five thumbs," that were ready and willing at all times to attack—whether it was work or some invader who had committed an infraction on the object of your interest—there was a heart beneath. There was a heart red with pure blood, unadulterated, affectionate, contrite, noble, sympathetic, tender, warm and zealous.

Your religious life was manifested in ways most unusual. You took great interest in the less fortunate. You spent much of your time and most of your money during the depression years feeding the hungry, clothing the threadbare and ragged, supplying fuel for the cold and unsheltered, and seeking jobs for the unemployed.

I have seen you even go so far as to bury the body of an indigent old man who had no one to put him away. Not too bad. This record continued will very likely get you in the gates by St. Peter.

In 1929 you stepped into the Manassas School, bringing with you in one small package all these attributes in addition to your unbounded ambition, steadfast determination, extraordinary tact, and a sense of duty blind to the exhaustion of work.

On that hot sunshiny September day in 1929, when you rushed excitedly into Manassas School to assume the job that would be the crowning point of your life's work, your words were stern and to the point. Your assignments were unlimited. Your days were long and hard. The job was tough. The parents were critical and quarrelsome. The children were unruly. This was evidenced by XX-boy's mother who came over with her shotgun because you had corrected her son.

It will well be remembered how you caught and confiscated the "44" from J. B., whose mother came over to fight and finally ended up really fighting. But the fight was between her and her son, J. B. It is almost unbelievable how you had to break up shooting craps on the school campus and up and down the street, then called "White Street" in front of the school; how you had to patrol the yards at night to keep down crime during concerts and meetings at the school.

Nor is this the half. 'Through the Years with J. Ashton Hayes,' that quarter of a century was filled with every thinkable type of problem that could arise in a community.

Finally a gradual change took place. After about ten years, fist fights just about disappeared, and pistols and knives became passé. The community took on new modes of living, less crime persisted, and the school had a new meaning.

The stucco building on the corner of Manassas Street and White had seen its best days. The more than 1,200 students, then attending Manassas School, wore their coats and hats in the classroom in order to keep warm. Toilet facilities were limited and unsanitary. The cafeteria was upstairs in a little frame building (constructed by Mrs. Taylor and her boys) where they served neckbones and dressing for five cents. This is where you sent them each day after the 11:20-to-12:00 devotions in the auditorium, and after they had sung for you a song that you taught them the first day you came to the school—'Soup, Soup, We All Like Soup,' sung to the tune of 'Hail, Hail, the Gang's All Here.'

Before there was money available to construct new buildings, you were bidding for relief at Manassas School. The auditorium, which was the last great job of your predecessor, was the only building on the grounds that was not a hazard in every sense of the word. You invited

Mr. Elihu E. Teague

persons from the 'powers that be' to look the situation over. One of the little tricks you pulled had to do with overcrowded conditions. On one of these inspection tours with officials, you had the children sit two and three to a seat in a room. By the time the guest reached the next room via the halls, the pupils had beaten them there by going around the house and had crowded out and congested that room. The 'powers' marveled at the terrible conditions. This went on until they sent you some relief, in the form of the first annex to the auditorium. And finally things grew increasingly better, and the school grew with them.

With the coming of better school facilities, you continued to alter your program in keeping with the pace and time. You brought out the best speakers. Any outstanding persons visiting in Bluff City, you saw to it that Manassas pupils were exposed to them. You always announced your motto: 'The Best Is None Too Good for Manassas.'

Through the years, J. Ashton Hayes, you had by your side a little man, loyal, faithful, and true. Once he took the faculty by surprise by losing his temper—never before witnessed by them of Elihu A. Teague. He was a leavening agency for your very opposite disposition and actions. As your assistant, he backed you in everything—right or wrong, thick or thin—and things never became too thick for him to stick. Tonight he sits dramatically by to watch with you, and with us, events as they close your career at Manassas School.

At this point, the writer told of many experiences which she had encountered as the first secretary to Mr. Hayes. Among these it was cited that he had directed hundreds of letters to Mr. Clifford Reynolds, then director of personnel at the Firestone Tire and Rubber Company plant, which was across the street and a little distance away to the right of the Manassas School buildings. At the time of this ritualistic occasion for Mr. Hayes, Mr. Reynolds was no longer living.

After the dedication of a poem—"I Live for Those Who Love Me," by Mrs. Bernice Thomas, an outstanding teacher in the school, the narration continued:

Then, J. Ashton Hayes, you had a secretary to succeed me, who remained only one year. But one succeeded her who is here tonight.

Miss Maggie L. McDowell

Maggie graduated at Manassas High School, received her B.S. degree in Business Education at Tennessee State University, her M.Ed. in office management and business education at Memphis State University, with further study also done at Memphis State University.

33

Her work experience included performing the duty of secretary-treasurer at Manassas High School; first business education teacher at Melrose High School; first of two vocational office education teachers; and at present cooperative office education coordinator at Melrose High School.

Her professional duties by no means occupied all her time. She also devoted her efficient services to her religious and civic life. She stated: "I believe that my early training at home, church, and school made the difference in my striving for an opportunity to serve mankind. The basic foundation in my life was laid layer on layer, at these three places. There really can be no success in one's life unless one is dedicated to helping, inspiring, and believing in others."

So it was with this philosophy of life that Maggie L. McDowell began her services, along with her professional duties for others.

She worked on the board of directors with the Mental Health Association, and the board of directors of the Nurses' League. At present she is serving as member-at-large with the Mid-South Medical Association. She served as regional director of Delta Sigma Theta Sorority from 1961 through 1965, and was a member of the National Nominating Committee of the sorority in 1967.

As a devout and staunch member of her church (Trinity Christian Methodist Episcopal) she served in many capacities; a regular member of the Sunday School, financial secretary of the school, member of District Laymen's Group, and public relations chairman of the Church.

(Narration continues)

Miss McDowell began working in your office when she was in the ninth grade, helping as an office girl. After graduation she spent two or three years at Tennessee State College, during which time she was called to return to Manassas School as the secretary to her former principal. This was not too difficult a decision to make, because

Maggie was one of three daughters of a widowed mother and the scuffle was too hard for the family to keep up. She became an almost indispensable part of the Manassas setup. But no one likes to stand in the way of progress, and so she completed her education during her summers and became a teacher in the Memphis school system. It was like pulling your eyeteeth to see Maggie leave, particularly if you had had any eyeteeth.

Yes, Maggie was a favorite student graduate of Manassas High School. In fact all students who go out into the world after graduation and make good are favorites with you.

It would be pretty difficult to bring to your attention the quarter of a century of work done by you in a few hours, so consequently I shall now focus attention on another phase of your life.

At this point I should like to name those who lived with you through it all—running when you ran, weeping when you wept, and smiling when you smiled. I have already called the name of the man who was attached to your side, Elihu A. Teague. But there were others too. When you walked in you found them here, and when you walked out you left them here: Willia Alma McWilliams, Georgia R. Sylvers, Ethel J. Perkins, Bebe C. Fingal, Rubye Berry Jones, Deanie Banks Johnson, Frances Tharpe, Bernice Thomas, Emanuel Weed, Emma Johnson, and your narrator—Addie D. Jones. Others came and went, and still others came and stayed, but all added to the sum total of your inspiring efforts and enthusiastic ventures. Anyway, like all great undertakings, there is a crowning point.

There is another side to your life that we have not pointed up as yet, which was one of the greatest virtues a man may be able to possess—and that is family life. One-half of your success as a gentleman may be attributed to the rearing of two fine children, Flora Mae and Pinckney.

Flora Mae, the fairest rose in your garden, was a miniature James Ashton Hayes, who brought a sort of pride to you that satisfied your inner being because you were both father and mother to her. By the same token, I guess, you are both grandfather and grandmother to Flora's offspring.

When you had weathered your two children over the dangers of youth and satisfactorily equipped them with weapons to fight their own battles in life, a new and inspiring note struck your life. Well timed, it was, made to order in disposition, tact, and the characteristics which tend to sweeten the fruit at maturity, your beloved wife, Rosalind, appeared on the scene and fate ordained it so. A new page was written into your history and a sense of satisfaction seemed to have been experienced, and your happiness seems complete.

When you had laid the last brick on your structure, at which you had labored so long, you then looked around for the man you could recommend to succeed you. It so happened that you knew him, knew his capabilities, knew his strengths, his passionate love for the education of youth and his understanding of their characteristics. You knew of his marvelous ability of self-control and that he is a brilliant scholar, a devout Christian, truly prepared to carry on a great program of education. Knowing these things, you felt certain that he was the proper person to take on so precious a heritage.

And so the brilliant young scholar, Louis B. Hobson, prayerfully and thoughtfully took over, and his performance will be reflected in the forthcoming pages of this history.

LOUIS B. HOBSON, PRINCIPAL OF
MANASSAS HIGH SCHOOL SINCE 1952

The walls of his office are decorated with plaques and citations for community service, all of which were well deserved for his dedication to human development and uplift. Such plaques were given him by the United Negro College Fund, March of Dimes, The Heart Fund, Boy Scouts, The Elks for community service, and the Pan-Hellenic Council.

Mr. Louis B. Hobson

Mr. Hobson came to Memphis after he had completed the 10th grade in the county of his birth, Fayette, Tennessee. He completed his high school work at the old Howe Institute. From there he spent four years at Virginia Union University and graduated *cum laude*. He received his first M.A. degree in social science from Western Reserve University, and a second M.A. degree in educational administration at the University of Michigan. Besides this, from time to time he has studied at other institutions including LeMoyne College, Tennessee State University, Memphis State University, the University of Tennessee, and Henderson Business College.

His work tenure began with one year at Roger Williams College. He began with the public schools of Memphis in 1934. He taught at Manassas High School until his career was interrupted by army service from April 1942 until August 1945. He served as principal of Lester Elementary School from 1949 to 1953.

Aside from the tremendous job as principal of Manassas School, he has spent much time working with the following organizations: Member of board of directors of Travelers Aid Society; Memphis Round Table, National Conference of Christians and Jews; Shelby United Neighbors and its Budget Committee, Advisory Council of Project Outreach; Little Flower Church; Catholic Scholarships for Negroes, Inc., Springfield, Massachusetts. Chairman of the following: City of Memphis Board of Electrical Examiners and Supervisors; board of directors, Memphis Urban League; Family and Assistance Panel II of SUN Budget Committee; vice president-in-charge of program the Serra Club of Memphis. Member: Catholic human relations council (one of its three founders); Little Flower Church Senate; Knights of St. Gregory; the Honor Society of Phi Kappa Phi; Phi Delta Kappa, honorary education fraternity; Phi Beta Sigma Fraternity, The Memphian Club, social, civic and cultural.

The Administration of Louis B. Hobson

When Mr. Hobson, the present incumbent, came to Manassas School to administer its program in 1953, the school was classified as a large comprehensive high school. He came in as the young man who could steer the school through its first evaluation for regional accreditation by the Southern Association of Colleges and Secondary Schools. Needless to say that evaluation was a success, and since that time the school has remained on the accredited list.

38

But the foregoing project was not his greatest problem. He came to the school when the surrounding community was changing in character and pattern, socially and physically. Small homeowners in the area were being bought out by the City Housing Authority and new housing projects were being erected. Tenants were moving in from many directions. There still remained, however, in a great number of areas of the community, many small dilapidated tenant houses—blocks and blocks of them. On some streets there still remained a few small homes owned by persons who desired to stay in the neighborhood. It was a new and different community.

This great change, of course, had its impact on the school, its operation, its disciplines, and the attitudes of the students and teachers. New and difficult kinds of problems began to show up. All this was not easy for Mr. Hobson. But he was seasoned with the hardships of struggles for his own education of two M.A. degrees and a number of hours unclassified beyond that. Too, there still were some veteran teachers there who were willing to cooperate in carrying out his plans of operation and to see that they would succeed.

As of September 1954, the school population was 1,919 students. The grades comprised first through twelfth. By 1959, some relief was offered by reorganizing the school and placing grades 1-6 under an elementary principal, leaving 7-12 as Manassas Junior-Senior High. Within four more years the elementary grades were removed from the premises to another school in the neighborhood and much relief was offered spacewise.

This new arrangement allowed more time and study to the development of his pet philosophy—scholarship and excellence. Each administration had the same motivations, the same hopes and avid determination to push forward toward the goal of helping an underprivileged people raise their level of achievement and productivity. Yet each held strongly to his own conviction as to the crucial problem at which he must expend his greatest energies. By the early 1960s it was clearly evident that an era of revolution was slowly but surely

39

approaching.

Mr. Hobson predicted many, many times to the faculty some of the kinds of things that might be expected. He was innovative, resourceful, and forceful in his convictions that Manassas students should be able to compete with students anywhere. So when the North Central Association of Colleges and Secondary Schools, through the Commission on Research and Service, submitted applications to the Carnegie Corporation for funds to conduct a project known as the Superior and Talented Student Program (STS) Mr. Hobson was one of the first principals who asked for it when it reached the Memphis Board of Education. This project was directed in Memphis by Mr. Shelby Counce.

Mr. Hobson immediately began the reorganization of the high school students. Indentification procedures were set up, and grouping took place early in the 1960s. All procedures were worked through committees under his direction. Motivation techniques were spelled out and facilitated. Levels of teaching were assigned to teachers who felt themselves most capable of handling certain levels of achievement.

Of course the three major issues of the STS Program were identification, motivation, and education. Under this program, enriched courses were developed commensurate with students wanting and needing such help. This help was selected from students who were members of the Future Teachers of America Club in the school. This organization also supplied classroom help for emergencies of regular teachers.

Efforts were made in 1959 (with the advent of professional counselors on the scene) to work with students who might have been considered as having problems, whether educational, economic, social, or personal. In these and many other ways high interest was maintained by many competent students.

Perhaps a great thrust in this direction was the achievement of one of our prize graduates. Napoleon Williams, identified early in the 10th grade as a gifted student, who stood at the head of the graduation list academically. He came through with a perfect score of 800 in mathematics on the College Entrance Board (SAT). His biographical sketch will be found under the heading of Men and Women of Distinction. His total scholarship offerings aggregated more than $30,000. He accepted Harvard's scholarship grant.

This was the beginning of a new chapter in the history of Manassas School, and it was again off to a swing upward in scholarship. Those with the ability to do so, worked hard for large offerings. The doors had swung open to blacks in the largest and oldest colleges in the country, and Manassas graduates led the parade from Memphis high schools.

It is somewhat difficult to measure the real value of the STS Program but a very definite recognizable change was in the number of Manassas graduates who went to college the years preceding participation and the years following the entry into the program. Too, it was the privilege of the principal to find, develop, and implement procedures and programs in his school which would best fulfill the objectives of the program. At this task, Mr. Hobson was a master. For the benefit of the reader as to its appraisal as of November 1964, the following is a report sent in to Mr. Counce:

We feel very strongly that the STS Program has been the greatest factor in the academic achievement of students of Manassas High School. This is our fourth year of participation, and we have noted some very striking results.

At regular intervals evaluations of our techniques have been made. Identifying instruments have been improved; new motivating ideas have been developed, and teachers are becoming increasingly creative in their procedures and adjusting them to the needs of individual students.

Conferences with the parents have brought them into the program with an increased understanding of their children's needs. On occasions of these conferences parents have evidenced an enthusiastic, cooperative spirit.

41

Classes—which are taught on levels, the STS Program being level 3—have been taken on field trips, to legitimate stage plays, and on other cultural excursions. Enrichment programs include literature, art, and music appreciation. Many of these students were recommended and attended summer humanities' institutes, and others attended humanities' institutes on Saturdays, during the regular schoolyear.

Frequent counseling interviews are held with students in an effort to help them with course selection, vocational choice, and transition from one level to another. These, together with their personal and social problems, have become a part of the entire counseling process.

In 1959-60, the percentage of the graduating class entering college was 28.2. At the close of the year 1963-64, the percentage of the graduating class entering college was 36.5.

On the basis of the above and other facts not mentioned, we believe that the STS program has been a highly motivating force for academic achievement in our school.

When the Advanced Placement Program made its advent into the Memphis City schools, again Mr. Hobson asked for the program. Many of the teachers had become highly specialized in teaching faster-learning students. This was particularly true with the mathematics and English STS teachers. So academically the topmost students were allowed to take advanced placement English or mathematics. Rated on the basis of Excellent, Good, Medium, Fair, the results could probably be rated as Medium or Good.

Several students were successful in getting a freshman subject waived. One student who particularly should be mentioned here would be Carol Branham, who went to Bryn Mawr. At first her score was not accepted by the English department there. But by the end of the second month, a letter was received to the effect that she was only bored doing freshman English and would be assigned to a higher level.

Holding together a black school during an upheaval such as took place in the 1960s was a challenge to the strength of the best of men. It was no less so to Mr. Hobson. One after the other, at intervals, revolts occurred either overtly or through some hidden undercover destructive act. Manassas students as yet had not joined the parade. Finally, as it was expected, they caught the spirit of the whole revolt and began to join in. This excluded many who had serious intentions and felt the urge to continue to devote their energies to the process of learning.

On two occasions they had witnessed the invasion of the school by two nearby schools with little results. On one occasion, Mr. Hobson stood in the midst of the riot-torn situation and ordered all Manassas students to return to their classes. No bricks were thrown at him, but two large burly football players came toward him and whispered to him, "We are with you, Mr. Hobson." How good could a man feel under such conditions?

Along with some others, I believe that one of the many reasons Manassas students did not join the social explosion earlier was attributable to a preventive measure which had been taken during the school year 1964-65.

True to his ability to foresee trouble brewing long before it came, Mr. Hobson launched an intensive study of the school, community, and students attending the school. This study became known as the Manassas Program for the Improvement of Learning.

In launching this project, Mr. Hobson appointed the following committee, all of whom were chairmen of their particular departments: Mrs. Juanita R. Turner, chairman of the project—Mathematics; Mr. Willie Ware, co-chairman—NDCC; Miss Lucille Fultz—English; Mrs. Katherine Thomas—Foreign Languages; Mr. Emerson Able—Music; Miss Ramelle Eddins—Home Economics; Mrs. Bessie Garrett—Business Education; Mr. Leon German—Social Science; Mr.

Walter P. Guy—Art; Mrs. Addie D. Jones—Guidance; Mr. Autres Plaxico—Science; and Mrs. Majorie Ulen, who served only until January 1965.

Other members of the faculty made reports at regular meetings on assigned subjects.

Here I am inclined to quote directly from the pamphlet, some passages which will give the reader an idea of the kind of work that was done during that study.

Page 3 of the document reads thus:

Acknowledgments

The work of the committee has been advanced greatly by the study of projects from other school districts. The committee drew heavily on the Higher Horizon Program and the Banneker School District Project. The members of the committee are grateful for these and other sources studied during the development of this project. They are also grateful for the discussions conducted by Dr. John Codwell, Codirector of the Southern Association's Educational Improvement Project, and Mr. James D. Marsh, Assistant Director Memphis Area Vocational Technical School, and all others who gave their help and moral support.

This committee accepts responsibility for the final form of this report, but it wishes to express thanks for the help given by its own members, for the assistance given by the special faculty committees, and for the continuing advice and encouragement from the principal, Mr. L. B.Hobson, and the assistant, Mr. R. Neely, Sr.

The Introductory Statement, as written by Mr. Hobson:

What we are calling the Manassas Program for the Improvement of Learning was not designed as a statistical research study. What we have done has been to take a look at the kinds of students that attend Manassas, the kind of community from which they come, and, calling upon our own experiences and the result of our study of promising

44

practices that have been used in other school systems and in other schools, have worked out a program that we believe will improve learning in our school.

The emphases in our plan are on what we can do within the present framework to do a better job. We are calling for some outside additional help, but not much. Our position here is not that additional money is not needed. We have reached the conclusion from our study that actually, in the same school system, the per pupil expenditures might need to be twice as high in one school as in another to establish and maintain equality of educational opportunity. In these schools there must be compensation to effect equality. But we believe that much can be done under the present situation. We have already gained new insight, inspiration, and increased knowledge from our study, from discussions, etc., on how to work more effectively with the kinds of children that are predominant in our student body. We believe our level of competence has been raised, and certainly our determination to create the best possible learning situation for our children here at Manassas has been enhanced.

Every teacher on our staff has had a share in this effort. These teachers have worked indefatigably. They have done so, I believe, because they have sensed the need for what we are doing.

This written report is the work of a special committee formed from our faculty. They have, from the beginning, worked diligently to produce this *Manassas Plan*. We sincerely believe that the implementation of his plan will greatly improve learning in our school.—Louis B. Hobson

A gist of this study will give the reader some idea of the findings and conclusion.

The statistics quoted on housing and income confirm that our immediate community is a highly poverty stricken, low socioeconomic area in a much worse condition than had been previously depicted.

These figures are based on occupants of substandard housing only. (Definition: Housing is defined as substandard if it is either 1) dilapidated, and 2) lacks one or more of the following plumbing facilities: hot and cold water piped inside the structure; flush toilet for exclusive use of the occupants of the unit, and either bathtub or shower inside the structure for exclusive use of the occupants of the unit.)

A Sample of Statistics on Pupils

Pupils entering 9th grade	No. of graduates four years later
489 (1959-60)	264 (1963)
593 (1961-62)	360 (1965)

Such figures were also compiled on withdrawal rate, truancy rate, class-cutting, tardinesses, and failures.

After the study of the statistical data the following observations were made: The majority of the students who attend Manassas High School are poorly motivated and come from homes with low incomes, one parent (often female-based) and overcrowded conditions. Such a background poses a problem for the school because these students do not look upon the school as a place too different from the home environment and find it difficult to adjust. With such attitudes, these students are not readily receptive to the program the school attempts to present to them.

These negative attitudes are reflected in the high dropout rate, low IQs as measured by test scores, low reading and achievement test scores, and high rates of truancy, suspension, and class-cutting.

The school recognizes that when its program fails to meet the needs of its students, the problems will continue to pose a threat to the school and larger community as well.

The problem (or task) for the school, then, is to find some means of surmounting these problems. Its chief task is to devise a program that meets the needs of all students.

At Manassas, the term "culturally disadvantaged" is used to define those students who are not classified as STS

(Superior and Talented Students) or Achievement Emphasis (underachievers). Inasmuch as programs have been organized for those students who are academically talented and those who are underachieving in grades 7 and 8, the school saw the necessity for adapting its program to the needs of those students who fall between these two groups.

After the objectives of the program were set up, the following recommendations for action were adopted by the faculty:

Motivational Techniques

The students who attend Manassas School are not too different from the disadvantaged students in other schools. Those students lack motivation inspiration, and the desire to learn. Their level of achievement is usually very low. In order to change these patterns of behavior, it is necessary to include in this program certain features which will serve to inspire these students to a higher level of achievement.

The committee recommends that the following be included in this program:

1. Invite outstanding graduates of Manassas School to speak to the students in assemblies.
2. Invite outstanding persons from the community to give inspiration speeches.
3. Discuss the school's program with laymen in the community so that these people can implement the school's program at the community level.
4. Make contact with leaders in the community such as ministers, operators of businesses, etc., to seek assistance in keeping students away from places that do not contribute to wholesome recreational experiences.
5. Seek dedicated teachers who have attitudes and dispositions to inspire students to high achievement.
6. Continue present motivational techniques such as:
   Honor Roll

Varsity Scholarship Team
Honors Convocation
Principal's Banquet
Scholastic Contests (both inter and intra).
7. Attempt to raise the self-image.
8. Relate what is done in school to real life experiences—something that makes sense to the student.

Guidance

Considering the school population to be involved in the Manassas program, the committee is of the opinion that guidance should be an integral part of the process for the education of the disadvantaged youth. A great majority of these youths came to junior and senior high school as reluctant learners. Obviously these children need more intense guidance than others with more trying problems.

The aims of the guidance program, according to the committee, should be:

1. To help these young people to raise their self-concept and feel their own worth as individuals.
2. To inspire them to elevate their levels of aspirations.
3. To assist them in acquiring a drive to learn and an inspiration to be contributing members of society.
4. To help them develop interests commensurate with their abilities.
5. To aid them in sensing an awareness of values that will lead to a more satisfying life.

To implement these aims, intensive studies should be made of each student and his special needs. Such studies would include:

1. Case and family histories.
2. Student interests.
3. Aptitudes and achievements.

4. Counseling with both students and parents.
5. Administration and interpretation of interest inventories and other tests.
6. An intensive use of anecdotal records and sciometric devices.

Experience had dictated that in cases where counselors' loads have been about a thousand students to one counselor, their services have been far too inadequate.

For these reasons the committee on this program structure recommends the reduction of the counselor-pupil ratio to not more than one to three hundred students. It recommends that at least one full-time clerical helper be provided. It further recommends that aptitude testing be instituted, and that standardized preprinted cumulative folders be made available for a record on every student.

Training of Teachers

It is the belief of this committee that the success of this program will depend greatly on the attitude and training of teachers. Certainly students in this program require a special discipline for education, and their success in the program will be determined, in part, by the teachers who train them.

It is felt that the average teachers, who are trained to teach average students, need special training for teaching the culturally disadvantaged. It is for this reason that this committee offers the following recommendations regarding the retraining of teachers who will work directly with the pupils in this program.

The committee recommends:

1. *Workshops*
    a. That the teachers be given stipends to attend workshops during the summer.
    b. That workshops be set up within the school with

certain selected personnel in charge.

c. That periodic workshops be held during the school year to help teachers continue to study and plan for the education of these children.

2. *In-Service Training*
This committee strongly recommends that in-service training be devoted to the training of teachers for this project.

3. *The Selection of Teachers*
The committee recommends that teachers be selected for this program on the basis of their interest, training, and experience.

Curriculum Enrichment

This committee feels that with modification and enrichment the present curriculum can be adapted to the needs of the culturally disadvantaged, and that activities be geared to their needs.

Based on this information, the committee makes the following recommendations:

Additional courses and instructors:

1. *Vocational*
Refrigeration and air conditioning.
Commercial cooking.
Salesmanship.
Electricity.

2. *Arts*
Ceramics.
Appreciation courses.

3. *Additional Instructors*
Cosmetology.
Special teacher for literature.
Special teacher for composition and grammatical usage.
Reading teacher.

It is recommended that provision be made within the framework of each subject area and within the class for enriched experiences so that students with special abilties and talents may be able to work as near their potential and capacity as possible.

The committee feels that a teacher should be designated to general enrichment and as resource teacher. This person would serve as aid to teachers in organization of activities, reconstruction of curriculum to fit needs of pupils, and selection and adoption of instructional aids.

Remedial Services

The learning patterns of the culturally disadvantaged student are such that requires special assistance and tutoring beyond the work of the regular classroom teacher. In order to help him in his efforts to achieve, the committee recommends that:

1. A clinical tutoring program in English and mathematics be instituted and conducted by selected teachers and special students.
2. A reading specialist be employed.
3. Reading laboratories and equipment be installed.
4. Library books (classics) adapted to levels of disadvantaged be secured.
5. A full-time attendance teacher assigned to Manassas.

Cultural Experiences

In order to enrich the pupils in this program and familiarize them with the best the school and the community have to offer in terms of cultural experiences, the committee offers the following recommendations:

1. That the school sponsor programs to foster appreciation of art and music.
2. The school discourage auditorium assembly programs that are not cultural in aspects.

51

3. That the school include programs in keeping with the observance of Armed Forces Day, National Music Week, National Book Week, etc.
4. That the school make provisions for visits to museums, concerts, theaters, movies, parks, corporations, and industries such as:
Memphis Museum
Brooks Art Gallery
Symphonic concerts
Operas and ballets
Front Street Theater
Guild Art Movie House

Audubon Park
Overton Park
Metropolitan Airport
Local banks
Local colleges,

(Others may be included at the discretion of the committee.)

Parents

Any effort to improve the learning of children could hardly be much value without some contacts with the home. It has been the experience at Manassas School that parents will respond to calls for conferences with teachers and administrators when inadequate educational progress is the issue. They will visit also for the adjustment of disciplinary problems.

This committee is proposing a continuing relationship with parents in which parents may feel a responsibility for the progress of the child's education.

The committee proposes that the implementation of these plans be delegated to a special committee composed of key members of the PTA, and faculty and counseling staff.

In reviewing other programs for disadvantaged children,

many have reported failure with parent involvement. But the Banneker School District in St. Louis reported success in this endeavor. The special committee for the recruitment of parents will rely heavily on some of the techniques used in the Banneker district. Hence some of the workshop materials which they used are listed here for use by groups of parents and teachers in the Manassas program.

The committee proposes that parent study groups be set up in small units from twenty-five to thirty, and recommends that the following materials be included for use in these groups:

1. Concern, on the part of the parent, that the child get to school every day on time and with sufficient rest to be able to do a good job.
2. Assurance that the child is provided with tools for studying in a quiet, well lighted place.
3. A determined effort to see to it that the child spends some time studying at home each day.
4. Plans to visit the child's teacher at least once each semester.
5. Plans for the discussion of the child's report card to compare his level of achievement with his possible level of achievement reported by his teacher.
6. An effort to make it possible for him to get books from the library as recommended by his teacher and according to his own reading pleasure.
7. Interest in PTA work whenever there is available time.
8. Volunteer help as chaperones for excursions.
9. Suggestions for other needed discussion topics.

Record Keeping

During this participation in the project for improvement of learning at Manassas, the committee feels it is necessary to review the school record-keeping procedures. In order to present a more accurate picture of the achievement or lack of achievement of students, and to relieve the teachers of some of their extra duties, the committee proposes the following:

1. The employment of a record clerk.
2. The use of student office assistants and/or parents to assist the record clerk.
3. The establishment of a record office with a file room.
4. The placing of cumulative records in the guidance office to facilitate the work of the counselors in making referrals or in placing students in the proper grades.

Evaluation

Since the evaluation of the project is to be a continuous one, the committee proposes to:

1. Test the students at the beginning of the project, and at various intervals during the tenure of the project.
2. Use the same test for each evaluation.
3. Vary the evaluative test form, i.e., standardized test, nonstandardized test, teacher judgment and/or questionnaires.
4. Compile the results of each testing for an overall evaluation.
5. Revise or alter any phase of the project if the need is indicated by test results or otherwise.

Many of the recommendations of the Manassas Program For the Improvement of Learning could not be implemented because they were not within the province of the school itself but a matter of Board of Education policy. But much seemed to have been gained by teachers and students by the implementation of the recommendations which could be implemented by the school. Teachers were very much aware of the needs, and used every possible opportunity to create methods of inspiring the students to aspire for quality education.

There are many ways of determining success with students. One was in terms of creating competition. For a number of years, Sears Roebuck gave two scholarships to Negro schools. Few, probably not more than two or three, had been won by Manassas students by 1953. The scholarship recipients were selected by the Board of Education.

In the 1953-54 schoolyear, Manassas School was again a loser. The last winner had been in 1946-47 schoolyear.

When Mr. Hobson became principal in 1953, he set out to see that some student from Manassas would prepare to win. Beginning with the year 1954-55, and every year thereafter until 1967-68, a Manassas student won one of the two scholarships. In 1967-68, Sears Roebuck changed the method. All Negro high schools were given a scholarship. The main criterion was need.

During the schoolyear 1964-65, the National Achievement Scholarship Program, under the auspices of the National Merit Program, was designed to extend scholarships to more black students throughout the country. The competition was among top black students alone, and winners were awarded $1,500 per year for four years. The first year Manassas won two of the scholarships. The second year three; the third year three; the fourth year two; the fifth year two; the sixth year one. It led in numbers of the Memphis Negro high schools.

Another very much coveted award is offered by Firestone Tire and Rubber Company to sons and daughters of Firestone workers. The criteria are very rigid. In 1965, two Memphis high school students were listed as winners—one from Kingsbury High School (white) and Rita Marie Gatlin of Manassas High School (black).

Again, in 1969, three Memphis high school seniors won—two black and one white. One of the blacks was from South Side High School, recently integrated, and the other from Manassas High School—Zan Lee Perry, who is taking her college studies at Yale University.

For the year 1970, three scholarships from Firestone were awarded to the region—two of whom were from Memphis, and one from Walls, Mississippi. The two Memphis winners were Linnie Mae Reed (black) of Manassas High School, now attending Pembroke on Brown University Campus, and Clyde Tillman of Treadwell High (white). The Firestone scholarship grants are worth up to $1,750 a year toward tuition fees, required textbooks, and up to two-thirds of the room-and-board expense during four years of college.

Among the many headlines in local newspapers perhaps the most prized one reads as follows: "Manassas Wins First Place in Freedoms Foundation Contest." Memphis *Commercial Appeal*, May 14, 1965.

Manassas High School was awarded the Freedom Foundation Principal School Award and the George Washington Honor Medal by the Freedom Foundation at Valley Forge. The public announcement of this honor was made on February 22.

The Principal School Award carries with it an expense-paid trip for a teacher and a student as part of the Valley Forge Pilgrimage. This pilgrimage was made during the month of September 1965. Although up to one hundred schools throughout the United States can receive the George Washington Honor Medals, only fifty schools in the United States can receive The Principal School Award during any school year. Manassas was the only high school in Memphis to win this distinctive honor for the school year 1963-64.

The pilgrimage tour includes visits to the historic sites of Valley Forge, Philadelphia, Fort McHenry, and Washington, D.C. The formal announcement reads as follows:

Freedom Foundation at Valley Forge, Valley Forge, Pennsylvania. The trustees of Officers of Freedom Foundation at Valley Forge announce with pleasure the selection of Manassas High School by the distinguished National and School Awards Jury to receive Principal School Award for 1963-64 School Program, as outstanding accomplishment in helping to achieve a better understanding of the American Way of Life.—Kenneth D.

Wells, President.

Added information was received as follows:

As a recipient of a Principal Award, your school is entitled to designate one teacher and one student to participate in the Valley Forge Pilgrimage later this year. In addition, your school will receive a George Washington Honor Medal.

Mr. William R. Mitchell, Jr., one of the instructors in social science at Manassas was the coordinator of this program. Although he is very modest and shies away from plaudits, he has distinguished himself as a teacher and as a creative and effective leader of young people since joining the faculty at Manassas. He serves as chief advisor to the Quiz 'Em on the Air team, which is one of the best in the city school system. (For two consecutive years, 1964-65 and 1965-66, Manassas team held Grand Championship among the high schools of the city as a result of their successful record in answering the Quiz 'Em on the Air questions.)

Because of his distinguished service to the school as a whole as well as being the "spark plug" in the Freedom Foundation Program, he was designated by the principal of Manassas as the teacher to make the pilgrimage with a student to the sites mentioned.

Other members of the faculty who aided Mr. Mitchell in this project were Leon German and C. Jackson, of the social studies department; Walter Guy and Jobe Walker, of the art department; Miss Shirley Finnie and Mrs. Marion Pride (both graduates of Manassas) of the English department; Mesdames Bessie Garrett and Marjorie Ulen, and Misses Ruthie Grant and Dorothy Phillips of the business education department; Jesse Wilson of the mechanical drawing depart-Mrs. Bobbie B. Jones and Emerson Able of the music department; Jesse Wilson of the mechanical drawing dpeartment; and James Harris and Willie Ware of the NDCC department.

Even with the foresight with which Mr. Hobson was credited he could never have predicted the extent of the damage the 1969-1970 crises could have caused. "Black Mondays" triggered off the explosions. Black Monday in Memphis was part of the effort of the NAACP and a Union Coalition which had set forth certain demands from city authorities and hospital administration.

At first students at Manassas School were reluctant to move in with the boycott. But the school invasions during the first and second Black Monday finally triggered off the emotions and get-with-it attitude of the Manassas students. For a time, schools throughout the city became a shambles.

Along with the effort, radio stations were blasting the incidents as they happened or as they had heard happened. This helped to panic the parents listening at home and made them rush madly to the school to bring their children home. At this point Mr. Hobson wrote excuses—in person—to all students whose parents had come to school for them. On two Black Mondays, perhaps, 70 percent of the entire student body was absent.

It would certainly be difficult to realize how school spirit dropped, and how unimportant learning became in the minds of the young people. Probably 90 percent of the students did not know just what it was all about, and cared less; but they did know that it was much better and more fun to revolt than to try to remain in school when so many others were in the streets.

For Manassas School, this particular incident undermined the very foundation that had been so hard to build during Mr. Hobson's administration. But the never-die spirit was still a part of the character of the principal, and he sent out an SOS to the citizens of the community.

"We cannot sit idly by and watch the dry rot of an institution that has so long been nurtured by the sweat and blood of so many black people," Mr. Hobson said. And he told of the bitterness and lethargy of the pupils, and the helplessness with which the teachers themselves were ladened.

In all fairness, everything that happened to the students could not easily be blamed on Black Monday. The desegregation in faculty members had its share in the processes that led to this bitterness. Many of the best black teachers were transferred to all-white or predominantly white schools, while most of the teachers who replaced them at Manassas were white teachers who were beginning their first year and thus were inexperienced.

Because of his untiring service to the community and to community service agencies, Mr. Hobson was well known and respected and so his plea for community help was immediately heeded. Manassas Unlimited, Inc., was the outgrowth of several meetings held at Manassas School, with representatives from surrounding businesses and industries, as well as educational institutions, service organizations, and also civic-minded individuals. Included were the Cook Industries; Humko Products; E. L. Bruce Company; Firestone Tire and Rubber Company; Pepsi Cola Company; Kimberly Clark Corporation; First National Bank; Memphis Hardwood Flooring Company; LeMoyne-Owen College; Memphis State University; Dr. Julius Melton, of Southwestern University; Mr. Frank Buford, Manassas PTA; Mrs. Jeanetta Brantley, Manassas PTA; Mr. James Treat, of First National Bank; Mr. and Mrs. John Harrington, of Vista; Mrs. Emily Jackson, of Memphis Board of Education, coordinator of volunteers.

Manassas Unlimited, Inc., bids fair to bring back to Manassas much of what has been lost in this generation of young people. The high interest and conscientiousness of this large volunteer group forebodes such prediction. The businesses and industries are furnishing the money to cover expenses for the operation and lending their expertise in planning the program. A full-time executive director of the program (a volunteer) is on the job every day to see that things go.

The following article appeared in the March issue of the campus newspaper of Memphis State University:

Manassas Unlimited, Inc., a nonprofit, privately funded organization established to promote the Manassas High School neighborhood, is seeking student volunteers to serve as tutors.

About thirty-five Memphis State students, most from the College of Education, have already signed up to donate an hour or two per week to involve themselves in a one-to-one relationship with underachieving students. Many more students are needed in the project, however, and Dr. Roy Walker, Assistant Professor of Education, who is coordinating the recruitment of the volunteers, says that any student in the university who would like to serve is invited to participate. Application forms are available outside Room 202 of the Education building or from the secretary therein.

In addition to Memphis State, Southwestern, LeMoyne -Owen, and Christian Brothers Colleges are also involved in the project.

If enough students volunteer, buses will be chartered to take the tutors from Memphis State campus to Manassas. Plans are for buses to carry students two days per week, but most of the individual students will only go once a week. However, students who so desire may go both days.

A group of people from Manassas Unlimited organization came to Memphis State last Friday to talk to those people who already have volunteered. Other orientation sessions will be held to prepare the tutors for their job. Mrs. Georgia Harvey, a counselor at the Manassas School, will serve as coordinator of the tutoring program.

Tutors and students being tutored will both be in contact with Mrs. Harvey to ensure the best utilization of their time. The students will have some choice in the subject matter which they will teach. The two major areas of instruction will be communication and numbers. Dr. Walker said that although the proficiency of the tutor in the subject material is important, this factor is secondary to a willingness to work.

The situation at Manassas is typical of the urban ghetto school. A large percentage of the students there are underachievers, but there is also a minority of outstanding college-bound students. The school has already initiated an innovative program in which the better students are working with the slower ones with great success.

The tutoring program is actually only a small part of the total program envisioned by the Manassas Unlimited group. The organization, sparked by a dynamic principal at the school, hopes not only to help the students academically but also to help them to become better citizens through job orientation and similar programs.

One of the leaders in this phase of the program is Mr. Larry Hilbun, personnel director at Cook Industries, who is sharing his specialized knowledge with the group.

The fund for Needy School Children is also involved in the project, and Mrs. Myra Dreifus, president of the group, is on the planning committee of Manassas Unlimited.

The program is not an official university project. But Dr. A. Ford Haynes, chairman of the Department of Secondary Education, has given the group his blessing. Dr. Walker is involved as an individual and hopes to build interest in educational careers, promote relevance, and respond to someone's need for help.

A second facet of the program proposed by Manassas Unlimited, Inc., is aimed at the approximately 400 of the 7th grade students who will enter Manassas School come September 1971. As 20 percent of the entering class, as determined by past records, will be prepared for and motivated to benefit by the school's college preparatory curriculum, they will be placed in the standard curriculum program. For this group, special enriching experiences are being planned by Manassas Unlimited volunteers. These will include field trips, special lectures, films, and demonstrations, and a great-books program. No additional paid personnel or unusual extra funds will be requested for this program.

Again, on past performance, it has been projected that another 20 percent of the entering students will be found to be seriously impaired readers, unable to cope with the 7th grade curriculum because of their language and reading problems. This group will be tested and diagnosed by trained personnel for specific problem areas. Students who are at least three years below the standard median for their grade in reading and language ability but who are found to have the potential to improve will be placed in the special language study program, which will provide individualized help in developing reading and language skills. The Language Study Center will stress quiet areas for study, reading and testing, and will work with small groups for instruction.

Specific materials and books were selected by the education committee of Manassas Unlimited, headed by a teacher who had been trained in these special areas. These materials will form the beginning of the Media Center, a storage and disposal center to be administered by a librarian.

A remedial-reading teacher will serve as language studies director of the Manassas program. Her duties will extend beyond the Language Studies Center and into the new curriculum program for the remaining students, where she will help to develop a reading-oriented program. She will also plan projects and in-service training materials for the teachers in the 7th grade program.

The New Curriculum Program will serve the largest number of incoming students in the 7th grade (approximately 60 percent) and will encompass students who are average-slow as well as students three grade levels below the norm. It is believed that the vast majority of this group is teachable although lacking in motivation, interest, and self-respect. It is with this group that the major instructional thrust is planned.

The curriculum, which is now being organized by the education committee, will be coordinated into a unified program by Dr. Robert Kaiser, director of the Reading Center at Memphis State. Dr. Kaiser, as director, will have the esources of graduate students from Memphis State University. Specialists in mathematics, science, English, and history, who have been consulted in the content design, will also be involved in the in-service training of teachers and tutors and in some instances will work directly with the children.

It is planned that the director will build the curriculum, interrelate materials, and, together with the language studies director, will consult with the teachers both on a unit planning basis and a daily basis, to keep the program content fully integrated. Once the curriculum is established and the teachers are trained, it is felt that the position of the curriculum director can be taken over by the language studies director.

Parent-teacher conferences are incorporated as a most important part of the program. Initial meetings will be designed to explain the purpose of the new program and methods to be used. Small conference groups will also be arranged to allow parents more opportunity to seek information, and individual conferences throughout the year are planned. It is important for the parents to understand and support the program, for it is through their concern that the child can be reinforced in his new attempts to achieve. Their help in building good study habits, regular and punctual attendance habits, and acquiring a disposition to respect discipline, will be of great influence toward the success of their children. Attempts will be made to draw the parents into full participation at every possible level.

Mr. Hobson said: "There are so many areas of out-reach incorporated in this program, so many side effects to be hoped for, that some gains are inevitable."

Simply stated, the structure encompasses the instructional program, teacher education, and community involvement.

Mr. Hobson's entire tenure at Manassas School as principal has been spent consciously trying to prove that the disproportionate educational and/or cultural retardation of slum children is not the result of heredity but of environment. When he inherited this influx of students of this transit area in the Manassas vicinity he met a problem which had not been encountered by the previous principals. It was then that he set out to prove that environment was the prime reason for low IQs, poor school attendance, poor study habits, irresponsible behavior, and low self-concept. It was then that he determined to work plans that would salvage from that large group students who could be influenced to perform satisfactorily. He thus convinced himself that there is a high relationship between poverty and educational retardation.

Thus, through the years, his highly structured programs have been aimed at the development of the disadvantaged child. They have been designed to give lots of attention to individual students and/or small groups of children. About five years before this writing, a new school was built approximately ten blocks to the south of Mansassas School— all modern and with modern accommodations. It is called North Side High School.

At first the intention of the Board of Education was to move Manassas into this fabulous new structure and reduce the present Manassas School Building to a junior high or elementary. A petition was circulated by Manassas graduates, asking that the Board of Education not change the name of Manassas High School. And so much ado was made about it that the Board of Education converted North Side High School into a comprehensive high school, and Manassas was designated as a college preparatory school.

All vocational courses were moved from Manassas to North Side except some classes in home economics, some classes in woodwork, and some in shorthand and typewriting. When the boundaries were drawn for the two high schools, the Manassas boundary encompassed housing projects and many two- and three-room low-rent dilapidated houses in the slum areas. There could hardly be more than 3 percent of the homes in that vicinity owned by the occupants. This, along with the integration of teachers, mentioned elsewhere in this script, and the reign of terror that went along with it, brought into focus the new problem.

Throughout civilization, man has been prone to relish symbols of the past. He has spoken in terms of customs and traditions, and he has been inclined to hold on to them. This seems to be the kind of conditions which grip many of the graduates of Manassas. The terribly worn beige brick structure that houses the Manassas School is a symbol well known to the thousands who have passed through its tattered walls; and the greater their achievements, it would seem, the more sensitive they are to their feelings for its preservation. This tradition seems to give them a sense of belonging and a definite connection with what was an illustrious past begun and nourished by black men for black boys and girls.

Aside from a number of plans and program arrangements initiated by the several administrations—described elsewhere herein—there was a powerful intangible attribute to which success at this ghetto school may well be ascribed.

In the truest sense of the word, those who attended Manassas School were people and still are. They are sensitive to all the likes and dislikes, all the hurts and all the pleasures, all the joys and all the sorrows, and we could go on and on describing these sensitivities. But in reality this school was possessed of one very real thing that threw them out of the class of a truly ghetto school. The students were poor? Yes. Hungry? Yes. Ragged? Yes. Deprived and discriminated against? Yes. All these things, and more. But they felt the spirit that pervaded their lives in this ghetto setting—LOVE, KINDNESS, and the will to BECOME MEN AND WOMEN with a desire to go forth and spread these attributes and the joy of living!

There was beautiful educational rhetoric in the school philosophy probably as in most school philosophies. But it would have been of no avail without the sincerity of the dedicated black teachers to whom every black child, who came under his or her direction, was considered "a piece of gold in the rough." From rhetoric to action accounts for one of the differences between the much-discussed ghetto schools located in many of the largest cities in this country as well as the ghetto school in this theme.

So this is how the spirit was built during the early years, and carefully observed and guarded by each succeeding principal. This spirit became as contagious as any communicable disease. Probably nobody can write this attitude into a philosophy. But I firmly believe that although Manassas School is a school in the ghetto, it is not truly a ghetto school.

Over the years, graduates have written many letters to their former teachers. Not too many of the teachers took care to keep these letters because of space and convenience and, of course, other reasons. But one letter that happened to be available is included here. For reasons that permission to do this should be granted and other obvious reasons, the names are deleted.

Dear Mrs.————

It was glorious hearing your voice over the telephone the other night! It has been so long since I saw you or heard that lovely voice! As long as I shall live, I shall be obligated to you for the interest, help, and loving assistance you gave me when I was a poor struggling boy trying to work my way through Manassas School, so as to equip myself not only to make a good living but also to make a meaningful and serviceable life.

You spared no pains in challenging the highest and best in me. I saw in you the finest and best of Christian, cultured womanhood. The impact of your disciplined guidance and training on me impelled me to learn, labor, and dream of the better self I wanted to be. After all these years, I shall be obligated to you; and I shall strive to be a better man, lead a better life because of your influence on me.

Certainly when I come back to Memphis, I must bring my family. I have a very charming and lovely wife, who was a schoolmate at Lane. Having no children of our own, we have assisted in bringing to our home two nieces and one nephew, and we are educating them.

Since 1962, we have been bringing Liberian students to our home for college education. We now have some six in college—two at Tuskegee Institute, and four at Lane College.

God bless you in all your efforts. My family joins me in love and best wishes.

Sincerely,

Letters such as these could become a major part of this story of a ghetto school.

MEN AND WOMEN OF DISTINCTION

Club 41

In perusing the pages of black history one will find many faces that are not listed therein—faces of persons who so justly deserve to be included. Though dealing with a limited resource—graduates of Manassas High School—there will be listed some of the faces that so justly deserve to be placed in the history of our country. There will be seen many men and women of distinction. Not included will be a number of outstanding graduates of Manassas because of my inability to make contact with them.

This means that these people represent graduates who

have gone out from the school within the last half a century. As may will be remembered, the first graudation class was in 1924.

If one has read the story of the ups and downs of this ghetto school, it appears almost fantastic how its graduates could have worked their way to the heights which they have reached.

The graduates mentioned here are categorized as having been successful in various endeavors. These success stories include just good citizenship; the rearing of fine families; politics and law; the medical profession; athletics and sports; music and fine arts; education and teaching; industry and other substantial and respected occupations.

This picture shows a group of reputable and outstanding citizens of the city of Memphis, members of the class of 1941, who in March 1971 were able to attend the banquet representing their thirtieth year after graduation.

Seated at the banquet table, left to right—front row: Mrs. Bebe C. Fingal, teacher invited; Mrs. Bessie Lawson, member of club; Mrs. Addie D. Jones, teacher invited; Mrs. Georgia Quinn, teacher invited; Mrs. Ethel Perkins with her husband, she was a teacher invited; and Mr. Louis B. Hobson, present principal of Manassas. Standing, from left to right: Mrs. Kathleen Cawley; Mrs. Lavera Watkins; Mrs. Aline Upchurch; Mrs. Charles Erma Young; Mrs. Elsie Arnold; Mrs. Marie Macke; Howard Robinson; Mrs. Virginia Smith (resides in Chicago, here to attend the affair); Mrs. Johnnie Mae Taylor; Charlie Morris, Sr.,; Mrs. LaVerne Weathers; Ernest Withers; and Mrs. Julia Holman.

These men and women are listed as Men and Women of Distinction because, in their own way, they have, contributed to the community fine citizenship and reared fine families who are contributing. They are saluted in this "Portrait of a Ghetto School."

The president of the club, Mr. Charlie Morris, is a successful businessman. He is staff manager of the Memphis District of the North Carolina Mutual Life Insurance

Company; president of the Kennedy Democratic Organization; member of the board of directors of the Memphis Urban League; deacon of Corinthian Baptist Church; member of Klondyke Civic Club and its board of directors. He is married to the former Alma Gray, and they are the parents of three sons. Charles, Jr. attends Tennessee State University; Ronald graduated at Howard University and is at present working toward a Master's degree at Howard University; Anthony LaRoy, the youngest, is a junior at Memphis State University. The Morrises have one grandchild, Ursula Beatrice, four and a half years.

LAW AND POLITICS

EUGENE HAMILTON, Judge,
Superior Court of the District of Columbia,
Washington, D.C.

Judge Eugene N. Hamilton, Judge in the Superior Court of the District of Columbia, was sworn in on Monday, November 2, 1970, in Washington, D.C. Mr. Hamilton's nomination by the President of the United States was confirmed by the Senate on October 12, 1970.

Judge Eugene Hamilton

Eugene N. Hamilton, a native Memphian, attended school from 1st through 12th grade in the Memphis City School System. He was graduated from Manassas High School, where he was president of Student Council during his senior year.

After graduation from high school he attended the

71

University of Illinois, and earned his B.A. degree in economics and mathematics. After graduation, he attended the University of Illinois Law School, and earned his LL.B. degree in February 1959.

On active duty with the U.S. Army, he served as an attorney until 1961. During his service as an army attorney he represented individuals as well as the United States in the trials of various criminal actions varying from AWOL to attempted murder. In July 1961, Mr. Hamilton joined the Civil Division of the U.S. Department of Justice, and has been continuously associated with the Department until his appointment to judge of the Superior Court of the District of Columbia.

He is, and has been for some time, active in the construction and management of housing in Montgomery County for low- and middle-income families and for the elderly, and is presently on the board of directors of Great Hope Inc., and Bethany House, both of which are nonprofit housing corporations.

Mr. Hamilton is married to the former Virginia David of Wilberforce, Ohio. They have five children, Barbara June, John Steven, James Poole, Eric Eugene, and David Nolan, and all but the last two are in school in Montgomery County, and they reside in Silver Springs, Maryland.

GEORGE L. FORBES

Attorney George L. Forbes of Cleveland, Ohio, is a senior partner of the Gaines, Rogers, Horton and Forbes Law Firm. He has been a member of the Cleveland City Council since 1963, and is executive director of Minority Consultants, Inc., a consulting firm which specializes in the solutions to racial and minority problems in the urban areas.

George L. Forbes, Esq.

 Mr. Forbes was born in Memphis, Tennessee, and educated in the public schools through high school. He was a very much adored senior when he graduated at Manassas High School. He got his B.A. from Baldwin Wallace College, and his law degree at Cleveland Marshall Law School.

 Aside from his very busy schedule with his law practice and his city council work, he finds time to serve with the following community and civic organizations: Council for Economic Opportunities (in greater Cleveland); Cleveland Criminal Justice Coordinating Council; National Association for Advancement of Colored People; Glenville Area Council; and Forest Hill Parkway Civic Association.

 He also holds membership in the following professional organizations: Ohio State Bar Association; Cuyahoga County Bar Association; National Bar Association; and National Association of Defense Lawyers in Criminal Cases. In 1967, he was deputy campaign director for Mayor Carl B. Stokes. George L. Forbes is a busy man.

NAPOLEON B. WILLIAMS, JR.

So far as has been ascertained, Napoleon B. Williams, Jr., is the first student from Memphis to make a perfect college entrance examination board (SAT) score. He made a perfect 800 on his mathematics section when he was a senior at Manassas High School in 1960, and is the first black student from Memphis who is known to have graduated from Harvard College on complete scholarship aid from the college.

After his graduation from Harvard in 1964, he entered Columbia University Law School on a scholarship and graduated in 1967. Since that time, the brilliant scholar has been engaged in many varied activities. After his graduation at Manassas, he worked in the summer as laboratory researcher in physiology in the University of Tennessee Medical School in Memphis. During his 1962-64 years at Harvard University he worked as laboratory technician in genetics and in biology.

In 1965, during his summer break from law school, he was legal assistant and researcher for NAACP Legal Defense Fund, New York. He did part-time work at law school as legal researcher for Prof. Weinstein—now U.S. District judge for the Eastern District of New York. In 1966, Mr. Williams did research work for Prof. Curtis Berger at the Columbia Law School. He also was legal assistant in the Contracts Division of the Office of General Counsel of National Aeronautical and Space Administration, Washington, D.C. He also worked part-time as legal researcher for Prof. Albert J. Rosenthal of the Columbia Law School.

In the summer of 1967 he was consultant to the Human Resources Administration of the City of New York in the establishment of OEO-sponsored Legal Services Program for the poor in the city of New York.

During 1967-68 he assumed a full-time job as law clerk to U.S. District Judge Constance Baker Motley, in the Southern District of New York. In 1968-69 he was director of the National Clearinghouse for Legal Services, Washington, D.C.

At present, Napoleon Bonaparte Williams is attorney for the Carver Federal Savings and Loan Association, New York, with a multitude of duties to perform.

E. WINTHER McCROOM, Esq. At present in private practice in Cincinnati, Ohio, as of January, 1970.

Eddie Winther McCroom, young, brilliant, and determined, has fought his way up from the North Memphis ghetto to respect and honor in Cincinnati. In 1961 he published "First Look at the Ohio Civil Rights Commission," a critique on the Ohio Commission based on an analysis of the Ohio law as it existed at that time.

E. Winther McCroon, Esq.

He was listed in *Who's Who* among college and university students in 1956; was president of the student body at Arkansas AM&N College, where in 1955 he graduated with honors; and treasurer of the National Student Association in 1954-55.

Since his graduation from Western Reserve University Law School in 1961, he has served with distinction in the following places: he was appointed assistant United States attorney by Attorney General Robert Kennedy; appointed first assistant U.S. attorney by Attorney General Ramsey Clark; executive vice-president, Industrial Federal Savings and Loan Association; instructor at the University of Cincinnati Evening College; consultant to Department of Justice, Community Relations Service, 1970.

Aside from his work in his profession he has worked with the following organizations: vice-president, Citizens Committee on Youth; Alpha Phi Alpha Fraternity; Ohio Bar Association; American Bar Association; former board member and legal counselor to Cincinnati Jaycees; former state director to Ohio Jaycees; chairman, board of directors, Memorial Community Center (Community Chest agency); member of Budget Review Committee, Greater Cincinnati Community Chest; former advisor Cincinnatti NAACP; former legal advisor, Cincinnati and Middletown Chapters, CORE.

Mose Lewis, III, Esq.

MOSE LEWIS III
Attorney at law, Washington, D.C.

One of the Manassas High School's most effective Student Council presidents during his senior year (1955) was Mose Lewis III. He graduated at Central State College, Wilberforce, Ohio, in 1959, and did his army service during the years 1959-61.

After returning to civilian life he worked on several jobs including caseworker, Montgomery County Welfare Department in Dayton, Ohio; as correctional officer for Federal Reformatory at Chillicothe, Ohio; admissions counselor, Federal City College, Washington, D.C.; probation officer, Franklin County, Columbus, Ohio.

In 1970 he completed his law course at Howard University, Washington, D.C. At present, Attorney Lewis is principal legal advisor to the director of the OEO Office of Program Development. The program developed by that office consists of economic development projects, education projects, housing, communications, community development, and day care.

Mose Lewis' duties are reviewing grants and contracts issued by that office to assure compliance with the Economic Opportunity Act of 1964, and applicable policy and administrative regulations. He has represented the agency in inter-agency matters with the Small Business Administration, the Department of Agriculture and Department of Labor. In addition, he is a consultant attorney to the MATCH Institution, law firm of Jones, Jenkins and Warden.

He is married; no children as yet. He is a member of Omega Psi Phi Fraternity.

FRED DAVIS, Councilman
Now Chairman of the City Council

Councilman Fred Davis, both vocal and effective, elected to the first City Council of Memphis, has won for himself a

Fred Davis

highly respected place by his colleagues. From the Memphis *World*, June 7, 1969: "City Councilman Fred Davis last week won a victory of much needed park in the Orange Mound area he represents."

City Councilman Fred Davis, who is chairman of the council's housing committee, was a member of the delegation that went to Washington to present the case for Memphis' Beale Street urban development plan. Many believe that Davis' presence as a member of the city's governing body and well informed on housing problems, had a great deal to do with the success of the mission.

As councilman, Davis was also active in the efforts to prevent a disruptive strike by sanitation and hospital workers. He called for the establishment of a Human Relations Commission to work to prevent conditions causing riots. Effective and determined in these and many other efforts, Davis would be rated a man of top success.

Mr. Davis is a native Memphian, the son of Mr. Frank and the late Mrs. Charity Davis. His father was a North Memphis barber. He attended the public schools of Memphis, graduated at Manassas High School, and received his college degree from Tennessee State University, Nashville. Presently he is working on a master's degree at Memphis State University. He married a schoolmate from Tennessee State University, and is the father of three children.

City Councilman, Mr. Fred L. Davis, is the owner of the only black general insurance agency in the Mid-South. His firm is set up to cover life, health, homeowners, fire, bonds, and other kinds of insurance needed.

Fred L. Davis lived in the ghetto, worked in the fields during vacation time from school, and held other odd jobs to help put himself through Manassas High School.

MR. EDWARD E. REDDITT
A Symbol of Pride in Memphis

From the desk of Congressman Dan Kuykendall, the following article was released on July 7, 1971:

Senator Howard Baker, Senator Bill Brock, and Congressman Dan Kuykendall jointly announced today the appointment of Edward E. Redditt of Memphis to head a new central city community service office which will be opened in Memphis later this month. The primary function of this new office will be to maintain liaison between the three elected federal officials and various community service organizations. Mr. Redditt's office will assist in untangling many of the day-to-day problems which these organizations encounter in dealing with the federal establishment. This office will, in addition, handle a certain amount of the constituent casework for residents of the central city area.

Edward E. Redditt

79

In making the announcement, Congressman Kuykendall pointed out that "by virtue of his experience with the Memphis Police Department, and his involvement over the years with so many community organizations, Mr. Redditt is uniquely qualified for this new post."

And Senator Baker added, "Opening this community service office is something which Senator Brock, Congressman Kuykendall, and I have wanted to do for quite some time, but our biggest difficulty has been in finding the right man to direct the office. Our search for the right man is over, and I couldn't be more pleased that this project is finally getting off the ground."

Mr. Redditt, who is forty years old, was with the Memphis Police Department for ten and a half years, spending the last four years with the department's Police-Community Relations Bureau. A native of Ripley, Tennessee, Mr. Redditt was educated at Manassas High School in Memphis, and Lane College in Jackson, Tennessee, where he earned his B.S. degree. He served three years in the U.S. Army during the Korean conflict, reaching the rank of sergeant. Currently Mr. Redditt, his wife, Bobbie, and their four children reside at 1593 South Wellington.

There are probably few Memphians who do not know something of the work of Warrant Officer Ed Redditt. His office walls are decorated with plaques and citations from numerous organizations in recognition of outstanding civic work. His organizational affiliations include the People Power Project, of which he is advisor, made up of students from all high schools in the city, black and white, boys and girls; Shelby County Sesame Street, of which he is chairman, seeks to obtain TV sets for all neighborhood day care centers; Shelby United Neighbors; Kappa Alpha Psi Fraternity; leader of Boy Scout Troop 524; Memphis Track and Field Club, Inc.; Health and Welfare Planning Council; Neighborhood Referral; Aide of Memphis and Shelby County; LeMoyne-Owen College Human Relations Committee; Memphis Sports Action Committee. He is on the board of directors of National Conference of Christians and Jews; Porter Leath Children's Home; Memphis Volunteer Placement Program; Riverview-Kansas Community Day Care Center (he created the idea); The Memphis Cotton Makers Jubilee, Inc.; Chronic Diseases Advisory Committee; Advisory Council of WDIA Radio Station; Memphis Alcohol and Narcotic Council; Christian Brothers EPDA Community Advisor; National Family Service, Inc., and Tennessee Library Archives.

Volumes could be written about the help warrant Officer Redditt did in the inner city. On the occasion of opening the first Police Service Center he said: "Such store-front offices will bring the police into the community; will let the people get to know us."

He proposed the services of the center as: collection and distribution of clothes and food donated to the needy; health services, such as immunizations; family services and counseling; and providing a channel of communication between citizens with complaints directly to the appropriate City Hall agency, such as the sanitation or police department.

All the above were done, and much more.

CHARLES RUSSELL BRANHAM
Writer, Lecturer, Scholar

Charles Russell Branham graduated at Manassas High School in 1963 as valedictorian of his class. He won a scholarship to Rockford College, where he earned a Bachelor's degree in history. He continued with graduate study at the University of Chicago, Department of History, on a Ford Foundation Scholarship. He is now a candidate for Ph.D. degree. Currently he is working on his dissertation research. The dissertation is concerned with the nature of power or influence in the black community. What is attempted, here, is a survey of the relevancy of American urban institutions to black needs. "Since my professional interests studies and urban studies," says Charles Branham,

81

Charles Russell Branham

"my dissertation will demonstrate that the black problem and the urban problem are interrelated and will, in my opinion, demonstrate the relevancy of urban theory and urban history to the study of the black man in the United States."

Branham is working on two half-hour television programs covering the history of black Americans from Africa to the present. The series was scheduled to premier in September 1971, on WTTW-TV, under the title "The Black Experience."

In the summer of 1969, he was selected as a researcher for the Ford Foundation's Urban Negro in the Twentieth Century project. Two of his papers, "Oscar Depriest: Urban Politics and Black Leadership," and, "On the Nature of Social Mobility in the Black Community: 1945-1965," were selected for inclusion in the completed volume submitted by the project.

As an undergraduate at Rockford College he was active in campus affairs; served as president of both his freshman and sophomore classes and as Student Body president, also organized an abortive attempt to interest college students in the problems of the city's poor. The failure of the project only increased his interest in community work and urban problems, and he spent the next three years as a tutor in the Saybrooks project.

At the University of Chicago he served on the committee on African and Afro-American studies; was active in the Black Students Alliance; organized and spoke at the vigil to celebrate Malcolm X's birthday, and has taught at the Black "Communiversity" (without pay) at which place students learn without grades.

The twenty-six-year-old Branham has not married.

MELVIN S. BRANNON
Director of Urban League of Flint, Michigan.

The following article was taken from the Flint *Journal*, July 28, 1968.

The new executive director of the Urban League of Flint, Melvin S. Brannon, says he plans a 'more forward and aggressive movement toward involving people with the Urban League.'

Melvin S. Brannon

83

Brannon, 37, was appointed executive director at a meeting of the League's Board of Directors Tuesday night. He succeeds Milton J. Robinson, who became executive director of the Michigan Civil Rights Commission on November 2. Brannon has been deputy executive director since 1967, and served as acting executive director between the administration of John W. Mack and Robinson's last year.

Brannon said the 'New Thrust' concept of systems and institutional change through ghetto involvement and creative confrontation would be used to bring about change.

Before beginning with the Urban League in September 1968, Brannon was a counselor in job development and placement programs for the Flint Public Schools. Last spring, Brannon attended the National Urban League's executive development program in Washington, D.C. He was one of 20 men selected from around the country for the new program. Brannon's other offices are chairman of the advisory board of the Flint Regional Emergency Services, and vice-president of the Citizens Scholarship Foundation of Genesee County. He is a member of the Committee of the Urban Coalition of Greater Flint; COMPACT: the Service Center for Visually Impaired, and the Genesee Community Development Conference.

He and his wife, Johnnie M., of 1014 Barrington Drive, have four children.

Melvin's story could best be told by himself. After he graduated from Manassas High School, furthering his education was almost an impossibility. His parents were dead, jobs were scarce, and scholarship aid was practically nil. He would work awhile, when he could get work, and study as long as his money lasted. His only reason for being in Flint today was that he went there seeking work, and finally began to plant roots in Flint, and it became his home.

In 1959 he earned a diploma from the Hurley Hospital School of X-Ray Technology and then interned for a year in radiological technology in Arizona. He had done practically all his college work at Arkansas AM&N College, but still had not had enough money to stay there long enough to earn his diploma. It was only since he found substantial work in Flint that he returned to Arkansas AM&N College and was awarded his B.S. degree. He is a man with determination and willpower and prone to succeed.

Melvin has done college work at the Flint extension service of the University of Michigan and Eastern Michigan University.

JOSEPH WILSON WESTBROOK, Ph.D.
Area Superintendent, Memphis city schools

Dr. Joseph W. Westbrook is one of four Area Superintendents of the Memphis City Schools, and one of two Blacks. His entire public-school career was done in the city schools of Memphis, ending when he graduated from

Joseph Wilson Westbrook, Ph.D.

high school at Manassas. He received his baccalaureate degree at LeMoyne College; M.A. degree at Tennessee State University; and Ph.D. at the University of Tennessee, Knoxville, Tennessee. He is affectionately known by his close friends as "Joe."

His educational record is replete with study and work. He participated in summer workshops as follows: teaching science to disadvantaged students, Stanford University, National Science Foundation Institute on Teaching Chemistry; University of Wisconsin; Westinghouse—Science Teachers Conference on the Teaching of Science, Carnegie Institute of Technology, Pittsburgh; and The University of Colorado Science Supervisors Conference.

His work in education has been, as classroom teacher and athletic coach, fifteen years; assistant principal of senior high school three years; and superintendent of secondary instruction (he was the first Negro to hold this post) eight years. All the above were with the Memphis City School System.

He has also served as consultant for a number of conferences on teacher education and school integration, and was a consultant for workshops and conferences on faculty desegregation, school integration and student unrest.

At a recent meeting, Dr. Westbrook was elected president of the Tennessee Education Association. Term beginning in July 1972. He serves as vice-president of the organization at present. He is also a member of the National Education Association; Memphis Education Association, National Science Teachers Association; Association for Supervision and Curriculum Development; Phi Delta Kappa Education Fraternity; and National Science Supervisors Association.

Aside from his very pressing duties and heavy schedule in education, he spends some time in community service activities. He is a member of the board of directors of the Memphis Urban League; board of directors of Dixie Homes Goodwill Boys Club; Glenview YMCA; and member of tne Frontiers Club International.

Dr. Westbrook married Miss Dorothy Greene. They have two daughters, Mrs. Jolen A. Sawyer, and Jay Dianne Westbrook. They are also the proud parents of two sons, Joseph W. IV, and Capt. James Barrington (James was killed in action in Vietnam on August 25, 1968).

Paula Wooldridge

PAULA AND ROSE WOOLDRIDGE

From the 1966 graduating class there were three winners from Manassas School of the National Achievement Scholarship Program. The winners were Paula Wooldridge, Mary Robinson, and Thurman Northcross.

For reasons best known to them, Paula, her twin sister Rose, Mary Robinson, and another graduate of high standing, Rommel Childress, all four chose to attend Earlham College in Richmond, Indiana. Paula and Mary were on the $6,000 National Achievement Scholarship. The third winner, Thurman Northcross, used his at Weslyan University, Connecticut.

Paula went to Earlham with the intention of majoring in mathematics. But her advisor was a humanities major, and he strongly urged his advisees to take advantage of the opportunity for foreign study. Paula applied for a loan and a scholarship, and, in June 1968, was on her way to France.

En route she traveled with a group through Switzerland and then to France. For three weeks they settled in a small town in France and studied French conversation. From there they separated and went to work camps where they met students from other countries. According to Paula's story they studied for one month at the Institut de Touraine. In September they toured many parts of Europe. They were free to travel wherever they wished. After visiting nine countries, Paula and her companion wearily trudged back to Paris. They all lived in the homes of French families, and finally became adjusted to life in France.

After six months the group returned to Earlham, and Paula thought it very rewarding that they could converse fluently in French; whereupon the professor told her that she needed only two more courses for a French major. So in June 1970, she graduated with a double major in French and mathematics.

Paula worked as tutor-counselor for the Upward-Bound Program, as a library assistant, and an office helper at Earlham. Since graduation, Paula has earned fifteen undergraduate semester hours in education and six graduate hours also in education. She is presently employed as a mathematics teacher in the Memphis City School System at Sheffield High.

She has hopes that later she can take advantage of a scholarship offer at Cornell University sponsored by the Shell Corporation for achievement and merit scholars in mathematics and science.

ROSE WOOLDRIDGE

As an English major at Earlham, Rose was advised to take advantage of the foreign study program in England and Scotland. In order to meet all the requirements for a major in English, she chose Scotland. Her group was scheduled to leave one month before classes were to begin. So they also had an opportunity to travel in Europe. Later they went to

Edinburgh and enrolled at the university. Living in Scottish homes, they were introduced to the Scottish way of life. After four months in Europe, they returned to the United States.

Since graduation. Rose has been in a two-year program in English at Atlanta University where she is·an A student. Her scholarship specifies that she will teach in a college which serves disadvantaged students. She will apply for a position at LeMoyne College in Memphis, or Clark College in Atlanta.

EDUCATION

EDDIE N. WILLIAMS,
vice-president of Public Affairs
The University of Chicago

Eddie Williams is living up to his true traditional pattern of doing big things. He demonstrated these characteristics before graduating at Manassas School.

Eddie N. Williams

Mr. Williams is the vice-president for Public Affairs at The University of Chicago, Chicago, Illinois, and director of the Center for Policy Study. He is also a columnist with the Chicago *Sun-Times* newspaper.

After graduating from high school he attended the University of Illinois, Champaign, Illinois, and graduated with a B.A. degree in journalism. He has done graduate study in political science in Atlanta University and at Howard University at Washington, D.C.

He has held the following positions; reporter for the *Tri-State Defender* newspaper, Memphis, Tennessee, during summer school vacations; was managing editor of Memphis *Star Times*, a newspaper; radar officer and executive officer, U.S. Army Guided Missile Battery, March 1955 to March

1957. He was reporter, the Atlanta *Daily World;* Congressional Fellow of the American Political Association, Washington, D.C., staff assistant, U.S. Senate Committee on Foreign Relations Subcommittee on Disarmament, Washington, D.C., September 1959 to May 1960. Also he was research editor, Industrial Union Department, AFL-CIO, Washington, D.C., June to November 1960; Foreign Service reserve officer, U.S. Department of State, Washington D.C.; director, Office of Equal Employment Opportunity, and special assistant to the Assistant Secretary for Near-Eastern and South Asian Affairs, 1964-65; protocol officer, Office of the Chief of Protocol of The United States, 1961-64.

BESSIE T. BERRY

Mrs. Bessie Thompson Berry is the only black person to be a member of the Elmira, New York, Board of Education. Mrs. Berry stated: "Being the only black member has been a challenge, since it was a first in the history of Elmira and Chemung County. I was instrumental in getting January 15th as a school holiday in honor of the late Martin Luther King, Jr."

Bessie T. Berry

Mrs. Berry is the former Bessie Thompson, daughter of Mr. and Mrs. Benjamin Thompson. She finished at Manassas

School in 1949, and entered Tennessee State University in Nashville where she majored in business education. She dropped out of Tennessee State in December 1952, was married, and moved to Elmira, N.Y. She returned to Tennessee State in March 1956, and graduated with a B.S. degree in August 1956.

Bessie's employment: from 1961 to 1967 she was employed as a caseworker in the Children's Division of the Department of Social Services (commonly known as Child Welfare). In 1962, the State Department of Social Services recommended that a Protective Service Unit be set up in the local department. That challenge was given to her, the only black in the department.

In 1967 she transferred to the Chemung County Probation Department as probation officer, where she is presently employed. Again, she is the only black in this department.

The marital status of Mrs. Berry is "divorced." She is raising and educating two children. Theodore Francis Berry III, graduated at Elmira Free Academy, and entered Cornell University September 1971, to pursue a curriculum leading to architecture. Carmela Elizabeth Berry, a 10th grader, is a member of the Varsity Gymnastics team, specializing in Vaulting. She also is a member of the All-City Choir, Senior Choral, and a member of the Elmira-Corning Ballet Company. Both children are active in the Afro-American Society.

Mrs. Berry's further involvement includes being secretary of the Southern Tier Coalition, Inc., which is an activist group. The organization was formed in 1970 for the specific purpose of seeking out the identifying issues associated directly or indirectly with the inequities of life for racial minority groups. It works to resolve, in part or in whole, all identified issues, using established techniques and methods through direct affirmative action. She holds membership in the local chapter of the NAACP, and for the year 1971-72 has been elected president of the Chemung County Probation Officers Association.

MISS ETHEL SAWYER,
Candidate, Ph.D., Washington University

Ethel Sawyer finished high school at Manassas in June 1958. Being fourth of eleven children, in the home of Mr. and Mrs. Barney Sawyer, she was almost completely disillusioned. But through connections at Tougaloo College, she was able to get complete financial aid not only because of her need for this aid but also because she was an excellent student.

Ethel Sawyer

She graduated *cum laude* at Tougalöo with honors in sociology. Then she moved on to Washington University, St. Louis, Missouri, with scholarship or fellowship aid, where she was awarded essay honors in June 1965. Pursuant to her achievement of an M.A. degree she began further study toward Ph.D., and completed it with the exception of her dissertation.

Miss Sawyer's work record has included the following: research associate, Washington University, 1966-67; senior research associate, Tufts University—Delta Health Center, Mound Bayou, Mississippi, 1967-68; instructor of sociology, Haverford College, Haverford, Pennsylvania, 1968-69; instructor of sociology, Temple University, Philadelphia, and visiting lecturer, Haverford College 1969-71.

She was listed in Outstanding Young Women in America in 1968.

Dr. Edward L. Risby

DR. EDWARD L. RISBY

The following item was taken from a newspaper clipping:

Dr. Edward L. Risby, a former Memphian, who is director of the biomedical science program at Meharry Medical College in Nashville, has been recommended as one of America's Outstanding Young Men of 1970. The Outstanding Young Men program is sponsored by the United States Jaycees.

As a student at Manassas School, Edward Louis Risby showed earmarks of leadership, achievement, and success. In 1951 he won a book-reading contest during Boy's Week. He was a member of the Student Council, the Glee Club, and the track team.

After graduation he entered Lane College on a scholarship, and completed his senior year as president of the senior class; president of the Young Men's Senate; president of the Science Club; and member of the track team.

He received his M.A. degree at the Southern Illinois University in parasitology, and was the first Negro to receive a Ph.D. at Tulane. His doctorate was in parasitology and cell biology. For his paper he won the award over sixteen other biologists, who received Ph.D. degrees at Tulane during 1968-70.

Aside from his present position at Meharry Medical College, he taught at Lane College, Jackson, Tennessee, and Southern University in New Orleans.

Dr. Risby holds membership in the following professional, civic, and social organizations: American Society of Microbiology; American Society of Parasitologists; Society of Protozologists; Medical Committee for Human Rights; Alpha Phi Alpha Fraternity, Inc., and NAACP.

Edward Louis Risby and his wife, Elva Mary, are the parents of three: Emile, Edward Jr., and Rita.

EUGENE W. MADISON, Ph.D.

Dr. Madison graduated from Manassas High School in 1951. He attended LeMoyne College, in Memphis, majored in mathematics, and received B.S. in 1956. He received M.S. in mathematics from Michigan State University in 1958; was an

Dr. Eugene Madison

95

instructor at Fisk University 1958 through 1960; entered the University of Illinois in 1960 and attended through 1963. From there he went to California State College, Long Beach, California, and taught there from 1963 to 1966 while writing his dissertation. In 1966 he received his Ph.D. in mathematics from the University of Illinois.

Presently Dr. Madison is associate professor in the Department of Mathematics at the University of Iowa. His duties include the teaching of undergraduate and graduate mathematics and directing the research of Ph.D. candidates in mathematical logic. He was a visiting professor of mathematics at Yale University 1969-70.

He has written several papers in mathematical logic. Some of his writings are: "A Note on Computable Real Fields," published by the *Journal of Symbolic Logic*, Vol. 35, No. 2, June 1970; *Computable Fields and Arithmetically Definable Ordered Fields*, by A. H. Lachlan and E. W. Madison, published by the American Mathematical Society, Vol. 24, No. 4, April 1970; "Some Remarks on Computable (Non-Archimedian) Ordered Fields," 1969; and "Computable Algebra Structures and Non-standard 'Arithmetic," Published by Transactions, of the American Mathematical Society, Vol. 130, No. 1, January 1968.

Eugene Madison married Ethel Bell of Memphis, Tennessee, in 1956. They have three children, Sherryl, age twelve, Eric, age six, and Sabrina, age four.

MRS. VIVIAN O. DANDRIDGE-WHITE
MAT program, John Carroll University
Cleveland Board of Education

After graduation at Manassas High School, Mrs. White took her B.A. degree at LeMoyne College in Memphis. She began her teaching career in the Memphis School System. After one year she was married to Dr. A. A. White. To them a son was born, Augustus A. White, Jr. When her son was eight years old, his father died. Mrs. White returned to the

96

Vivian O. Dandridge-White

classroom at Douglass High School, and then back to her alma mater.

After she had taught for several years, during which time she was doing summer school work at Western Reserve University, Cleveland, Ohio, she moved to Cleveland. She began teaching in the school system in Cleveland, and after the second year was made chairman of the English department at Patrick Henry Junior High School. It was from this school that she was drafted into the Master Teacher Program at John Carroll University.

The John Carroll University MAT program is a joint project of the University and the Cleveland Board of Education. It is a very selective program for which students with a college degree may obtain an M.A. degree in education by training to teach in the inner-city under the superivision of a Master Teacher. Mrs. White began her services as a Master Teacher in July 1969.

There are several unique features of the MAT program. First, the students who enter the program are screened by numerous aptitude and psychological tests. Second, they are screened by a selection board through interviews and meetings where information is obtained concerning their backgrounds and attitudes to determine the probability of their success in teaching the disadvantaged child; and third, each student accepted must have a high academic standing.

Aside from an overwhelming success as a Master Teacher in the Master Teacher program, Mrs. White reared her son. This son is now an instructor in orthopaedic surgery at Yale University. He was selected as one of the ten Outstanding Young Men of the year for 1969 by the U.S. Jaycees and, among a long list of other honors, has been elected to the trustee board of his alma mater, Brown University. He is Dr. A. A. White, III.

Sallie C. Bartholomew

MRS. SALLIE C. BARTHOLOMEW

A very highly esteemed Memphis educator, Mrs. Bartholomew spent her entire life as well as her entire educational career in Memphis except for her graduate degree. She completed high school at Manassas, earned her college degree at LeMoyne and her M.A. at the University of Tennessee at Knoxville. At present Mrs. Bartholomew is principal of Orleans Elementary School. In this position, she has fought for the best in education for her young students.

She has spent thirty-one years of her career teaching in the public schools of Memphis. For nine years she has worked as an Elementary School principal. Among her other great contributions to society are her two children. The older, a daughter, recently received her Ph.D. at Ohio University; and her son, a fine artist in pursuit of his Ph.D. at Johns Hopkins

University. Her daughter did her undergraduate work at Howard University, Washington, D.C., and her son did his at Rutgers.

Mrs. Bartholomew still finds time to lend her help and untiring effort to community uplift and services. She is a member of the West Tennessee Education Association; Elementary School Principals, Tennessee Education Association; Memphis Education Association; National Education Association; Memphis Better Schools Committee; and Mental Health Association.

Among her memberships in religious and character-building organizations are Mississippi Boulevard Christian Church; Young Women's Christian Association Committee on Administration; the Trustee Board of the Memphis Pink Palace Museum; Memphis Chapter of Links, Inc., Memphis Alumnae Chapter of Delta Sigma Theta Sorority (a service organization); and the National Association for the Advancement of Colored People.

Mrs. Bartholomew is married to Mr. Caffrey Bartholomew, who has been a long-time employee of the Memphis postal system.

Ethel C. Brooks

99

MRS. ETHEL C. BROOKS

Principal of Alcy Elementary School, Memphis, Tennessee, Mrs. Brooks is very proud of her achievement because she entered the field in which she was profoundly interested. After having taught for several years, she was made principal of Wisconsin Elementary School from which she was recently transferred to Alcy.

She is married to Mr. Sylvester Brooks, and they are the parents of a son who is a student at Washington University, St. Louis, Missouri.

John Edward Wesley

JOHN EDWARD WESLEY

John Edward Wesley attended Manassas School from the 1st grade through high school. He knew and lived through the spirit disseminated at Manassas. He was graduated in 1947, immediately enrolled at Tennessee State University, and received his B.S. degree in biology in May 1951. He continued his education a year later, and attained his M.A. degree in 1960. Presently he is doing further graduate work toward a Ph.D.

He is principal of Lester High School. His experiences leading to this achievement were teacher of mathematics at Douglass High as a Junior High mathematics instructor after which he did his military time and returned to the Memphis City School System. He began as a teacher of mathematics at Lester High, from which post he was promoted to assistant principal and then to principal.

Mr. Wesley is married to the former Mary R. Robinson of Memphis.

MRS. CATHERINE D. BINGHAM
Home Economist, Federal Department,
Jersey City, New Jersey

On her graduation at Manassas High School in 1963, Catherine D. Bailey entered Tennessee State University from which place she received a B.S. degree in Home Economics in June 1967.

From August 1967 to August 1968, she served as benefit examiner for the Department of Social Security in Chicago, Illinois. In August 1967, she was married to Lewis Bingham (also a 1963 Manassas graduate). They moved to Jersey City, New Jersey, where they continued to reside.

Mrs. Bingham began work as a caseworker for the Department of Social Services in New York City in November 1968. In June of 1970 she was transferred, with promotion, to her present position of home economist within the Department of Social Services.

ANDREW GENE ADAMS

Good citizenship is one of the character traits that Manassas stressed through the years. Andrew Gene Adams went through high school from the 1st grade at Manassas School and never missed one day or was ever tardy. A young man with a perfect school attendance as well as a perfect citizenship record.

Andrew Gene Adams

EDNA MADISON WIGGINS
"Mathematics Wizard" was a nickname she was
given by her classmates at Manassas.

Edna's autobiographical sketch, unedited, is as follows:

Since graduation from Manassas High, I completed four years (B.S. degree in mathematics) at Michigan State University, and one year of graduate work at Southern Illinois University (where I also met my husband). I am presently married to Barry E. Wiggins, a native of Boston, Massachusetts, who is employed with IBM in Pomona, New Jersey, as a diagnostic scientific programmer. We have a home and three children—Deric five and a half, Carlos three and a half, and Tonilyn one and a half. Carlos is a child of mixed racial background whom we adopted two years ago. The other two are our natural children.

We lived in Boston for two and a half years after leaving Southern Illinois, where I taught for a while at Jamaica Plain High School. Then, because of my husband's job, we moved to Somers Point, a suburb of Atlantic City. I taught for one school year at Atlantic City High School before resigning to become a full-time mother of three small children.

I hope to be returning to a career after my children are older.

HAROLDINE BAILEY
First black student from Memphis to graduate
at Colby College, Waterville, Maine.

Haroldine finished at Manassas in 1966 with high honors. She was offered a number of scholarships from several big colleges, but wanted to go to Colby. Her scholarship there covered all expenses including a precollege institute and traveling expenses. She graduated in June 1970, with a B.A. degree and a major in English.

Since her graduation she has worked at Kingsborough Community College, is a lecturer in the Department of Student Services, and also serves as counselor intern. Her plans are to attend graduate school come fall of 1971.

MISS MAGGIE E. GIBBS
Airline Hostess, TWA.

Miss Maggie E. Gibbs graduated at Manassas High School in 1960. During her years there she was an excellent student in her content subjects as well as in art. She was a member of

Maggie E. Gibbs

the National Honor Society; a member of the choir; member of the *Newsette* staff; the Art Club, the Future Teachers of America, and the New Homemakers of America.

She entered Fisk University after graduation, and received her B.A. degree in 1964. While at Fisk, she was a member of the Art Club and Fisk Jubilee Singers for three years.

On leaving Fisk, she became the first Mid-South Negro to become an airline hostess. Presently she is employed by Trans-World Airlines as a hostess and line instructor.

"Marriage plans are in the making," she says, for a union with Mr. Harold E. Vann, who is the first black man to get a contract under option by the National League as that league's first black umpire in baseball.

CURTIS C. GARRISON
A first of his race.

Curtis C. Garrison, a very active student at Manassas School, participated in many endeavors. He was very much admired by his teachers and classmates for his scholastic achievements as well as for his attitude and willingness to work for any uplifting project.

Garrison was the first black man in the South to be permanently placed on the field staff of the United Rubber Workers International Union, AFL-CIO.

His job entails traveling all over the entire South organizing unions for the Rubber, Cork, Linoleum, and Plastic Workers of America, and negotiating new contracts on behalf of the International Union.

ERNEST WITHERS, JR.

Ernest Withers, Jr., an outstanding graduate of Manassas High School—as was his father, Ernest Sr., a well-known photographer in Memphis, who made the pictures used by Gerald Franks on the *Life and Death of Martin Luther King*.

104

Ernest Withers, Jr.

Ernest Jr. is director of Veterans Affairs at Federal City College, Washington, D.C.

Jacob Withers, also a Manassas graduate, brother of Ernest Withers, Sr., is a marshall in Washington, D.C. He was graduated at Howard University.

HOUSTON ANTWINE
Pro-football Star

The autobiographical sketch of Houston Antwine is copied below and is not edited because he is telling the story as it is, both good and bad.

I was born in Louise, Mississippi, April 11, 1939. My father was Joseph Antwine, Sr., and my mother is Evelyn Antwine. I have a brother Joseph, Jr.

We moved to Memphis when I was about three years of age. For more than ten years we lived in a community in North Memphis called 'Bear Waller.' If you know anything about Memphis, I need not say more about that area. Caldwell elementary school was where I spent the first five years of my formal education. Only five years were spent there due to the fact that there were only five grades to the school. I attended Grant School from the 6th through the 8th and entered Manassas School, where I finished 12th grade.

At Manassas, I became interested in football and tried out for the team and made it. After graduating, I accepted a scholarship at Southern Illinois University, played football, and accidentally started wrestling, and won the N.A.I.A. heavyweight championship; made Little All-American M.V.P. and captained the team my senior year in college.

Upon graduating from Southern with a B.S. in Education, I was drafted by Detroit of the NFL and Houston of the AFL. How I came to Boston is a story in itself, but Boston is where I ended up as a defensive tackle of the now Bay State Patriots.

Ten years of Pro-football has been wonderful to me. During that time, I have been All Pro for four years and I have participated in the AFL Pro-Bowl seven times. For the past two years, I have been the defensive captain of the Patriots and player representative. The most cherished of these honors would have to be my selection to the All-Time AFL team which is in the Hall of Fame in Canton, Ohio.

Along with football, I am currently in the life insurance business. With a brief venture in men's knitted outer wear, I have been in insurance business for the past six years.

I am married, and my wife and I have a little girl six years old. We chose to buy a home in Lexington, Massachusetts, where the three of us are living.

MRS. RHYNETTE NORTHCROSS-HURD

An outstanding Manassas student was graduated in 1967. Her very active school life did not deter her from maintaining high scholarship. Among the many scholarships she won was one from Mount Holyoke, which she accepted. She was a finalist in the National Achievement Scholarship Program; a member of the Varsity Scholarship Team, Mu Alpha Theta National Mathematics Club; National Honor Society; band member during her freshman and sophomore years; member of the Latin Club; and on the yearbook staff.

Her nonscholastic activities included NDCC Sponsor;

Deburette and Double Ten Social Clubs.

At Mount Holyoke College, Rhynette continued her activities. During her freshman year she won an English award (Merrill prize for work in freshman English). she was treasurer and social chairman of Afro-American Society during her freshman through junior years; member of Mount Holyoke Legislature (SGA); member of the multiracial committee; and a member of the Four-College Summer Program Planning Committee.

At Holyoke, her major was English composition and her minor was mathematics. Of course she got married. Her husband took her to Massachusetts, and she continued her studies at Simmons College in Boston. She received her B.A. degree from Mt. Holyoke in June 1971. She also received a fellowship from Harvard University to work on her master's in English and education. Her plans are to teach, and perhaps to pursue a career in writing.

She was married on June 6, 1970, to William C. Hurd, who was graduated at Manassas in 1965.

At the time of this publication, she is at Harvard on her above mentioned scholarship.

WILLIAM C. HURD
Scholar and Athlete

During his brilliant career at Manassas High School, William Hurd was a mathematics "whiz" to the students in his classes as well as to his teachers. Because of athletic prowess and his high scholarship, he exceeded anyone in his class in the number of scholarships he was offered. Among colleges offering them were MIT; Notre Dame; West Point; Southern California; Weslyan; and many others. He accepted one from Notre Dame for reasons that might be obvious—he might have been able to get a try for the Olympics.

At Notre Dame he majored in electrical engineering, graduated *cum laude*. His activities included being captain of track team, member of jazz orchestra, member of Afro-American Society, and secretary of Eta Kappa Nu (honorary electrical engineering society). Among his college awards were Rhodes Scholar semifinalist, scholar athlete award in senior class; athlete of the year at Notre Dame in 1968; holder of an American Indoor (300) yard dash record made in April 1968. He missed the 1968 Olympic team by one man.

After becoming interested in electric control systems and computers he worked for General Electric for one year, August 1969-70, as engineer and programmer, at G.E. Aircraft plant located near Boston.

Hurd returned to school and at present is working on his M.A. degree at MIT in management information systems and operations research.

Quoting Hurd:

I intend to use educational training and skills along with industrial experience to eventually help manage the financial aspects of black businesses in Memphis. It is my hope to use whatever personal contacts I have in the black communities in Memphis at an attempt to provide some of the feasible alternatives to the typically black consumer concerning goods he would otherwise buy from the white counterpart, such as clothing, housing, food, or other necessities.

I feel that Memphis particularly, compared with other major United States cities, has noticeably lacked this kind of businesslike (or managerial) leadership among blacks, perhaps because of the shortage of industry and partially because most of those blacks capable of setting examples in leadership areas of politics, business, or the like, seem to leave Memphis and are never heard from again after college.

Too, I intend to try for the '72 Olympic Games in Munich, and plan to continue playing music professionally.

The following is a clipping from a Notre Dame periodical:

108

On March 23, 1978, Notre Dame's Bill Hurd flashed across the finish line in the Western Michigan Relay's 300-yard dash in the American indoor record time of 29.8, besting what was probably the nation's finest assemblage of 300-yard sprinters, at Kalamazoo. Hurd clipped two-tenths of a second off the previous mark.

For the junior from Memphis, Tenn., the 29.8 clocking in the 300 is only one of many performances that rate him Notre Dame's Hallmark sprinter.

Hurd enrolled at Notre Dame in September of 1965 as a highly touted prep athlete credited with a wind-aided 9.3 100-yard performance at Manassas High School in Memphis. As a freshman, Hurd finished second to George Anderson, National AAU 100-meter champ in the Michigan AAU Meet's 60-yard dash in 06.1, and two weeks later claimed a victory in the 60-yard dash at the Michigan Federation Meet at Kalamazoo, establishing new meet, fieldhouse, and Notre Dame freshman records with a 06.0 clocking. At the National Federation Championships in New York, Hurd placed second behind three-time NCAA champion Charlie Greene in 06.2.

Hurd's best cinder performance came in his debut at the Kentucky Relays, when he set a meet record in the 100-yard dash qualifying even with a 09.5 only to place second in the same time in the finals.

Hurd was a superb indoor performer in 1968, copping first-place awards in his first five of six 60-yard dash starts. At the ICAA Meet in New York, Hurd captured the 60-yard title with a 06.2 clocking.

In addition to his track efforts, Hurd is a gifted musician. As a freshman, Hurd was named the "Outstanding Young Performer" in Notre Dame's Collegiate Jazz Festival, and was awarded a summer scholarship to the Music Conservatory at the California campus at Berkeley.

A Dean's List student since his first semester at Notre Dame, Hurd is majoring in enginerring at the University with a 3.4 grade average.

109

Dorothy M. Hollowell

MRS. DOROTHY MORGAN HOLLOWELL

Gets Danforth Postgraduate Fellowship. The following is a clipping from a New Haven paper:

Mrs. Dorothy M. Hollowell has been awarded a Danforth Postgraduate Black Studies Fellowship by the Danforth Foundation of St. Louis, Mo. She has received a stipend from the foundation to undertake participation in African and Afro-American studies at Yale University for the academic year of 1971-72.

Mrs. Hollowell is an instructor of English at the University of New Haven. She will be taking a leave of absence to complete her course.

She teaches studies in 20th century black novelists, survey of black literature, composition and literature, and world literature.

Mrs. Hollowell received her bachelor's degree from LeMoyne College, her master's from Atlanta University. She has also studied at Harvard University and will be going to Yale next year.

She is married to David A. Hollowell of Memphis. He is presently a full-time student at Yale and works part-time as an adjunct special lecturer in industrial engineering at the University of New Haven.

DAVID A. HOLLOWELL
Student at Yale University

The autobiographical sketch, unedited, is related in David's own composition for obvious reasons:

After leaving high school in 1963, I attended the Data Processing Institute (now renamed the State Technical Institute) and was among, along with my brother, Orenzo, the first group of blacks to attend this school. I graduated in 1965 and during the first year was selected to work at the Memphis City Board of Education building as a machine operator, by virtue of my scholastic achievement. Immediately after finishing this two-year program, I left Birmingham and obtained my first full-time job with the Union Circulation Company as a book salesman. In the fall

David A. Hollowell

I transferred to the Topeka Office and traveled to cities in Kansas, Iowa, Nebraska, South Dakota, and Minnesota, staying with this until November 1965. I then went to Minneapolis and took a job with the Gold Bond Stamp Company as a computer programmer.

I worked there until February of 1966, when I was drafted into military service. In the army I was assigned as a computer programming specialist with the Fort Belvoir Data Processing Center dealing with applications in finance and logistics. Later, I was assigned to the U.S. Army Engineer School as a senior programmer and systems designer to computerize their training programs using the facilities of the Interdepartmental Computer System at the Washington, D.C. City Government office building.

After being released from active duty in February 1968, I joined the Olin-Mathieson Chemical Company in New Haven, Connecticut, as a computer system analyst. After working for this company for a while, I felt obligated to return to school. I applied to and was given a scholarship by Yale University and upon notification of my admission, resigned my position at Olin and went to Atlanta, Georgia, to do volunteer work in the spring and summer of 1969.

When I entered Yale in September, I was selected to participate in the Directed Studies Program, an intensive program for 75 highly motivated freshmen, and I am still a part of that program in my sophomore year.

I am also working part-time as a special lecturer at the University of New Haven (formerly New Haven College) and serving occasionally as a tutor for transitional students at that school.

As for my future plans, I expect to graduate in 1973 and apply for admission to medical school, or some graduate school in my major field.

My wife, also a Manassasite, is the former Dorothy J. Morgan.

Carol Branham   Cathryn Branham

THE BRANHAM TWINS

Carol and Cathryn Branham were identical (not even identifiable individually) at the time they graduated at Manassas in 1965. They were competitors scholarshipwise.

The following article was taken from the Memphis *Commercial Appeal*, April 1965 edition:

Headline: TWIN SISTERS AT MANASSAS WIN SCHOLARSHIPS TO MATCH.

Cathryn and Carol Branham smiled proudly yesterday at their $6,000 national scholarships—as identical as the twins look.

The sisters, 17-year-old seniors at Manassas High School, were awarded the twin scholarships by the National Achievement Scholarship Program for outstanding Negroes after nationwide testing.

Two other Memphis students also received scholarships. They are Krystal Coleman of Melrose High School, and Elijah Noel at Father Bertrand High.

Winners, announced yesterday, were survivors of competition started last fall with 4,200 students from 1,300 high schools. The program is part of the National Merit Scholarship Corporation.

The Branham twins are the daughters of Mr. and Mrs. C. E. Branham. Mrs. Branham is a second-grade teacher at Caldwell Elementary School. A son, Charles Branham, is a student at Rockford College, Illinois, on scholarship.

Despite their matching scholarships, the girls staunchly say they are different. 'For twins, we have always been pretty independent. We think differently, but sometimes it comes out sounding the same,' said Carol. She is the younger of the two by seven minutes.

'Being twins has it disadvantages,' said Cathryn. 'People tend to think of you as one. It keeps people from knowing you as a person.'

Cathryn completed her B.A. degree at the University of Chicago and is at present in the doctoral program there. Carol completed her undergraduate work at Bryn Mawr, and is now in the graduate program at the University of Pennsylvania.

After four years in separate situations, it is evident that their personalities are somewhat different. And this is what they wanted.

LARRY ALBERT JONES
In five years med. program at Johns Hopkins
M.D. 1975.

Graduated at Manassas in 1967 was one of the National Achievement Scholarship winners. The other two were Francine Guy, and Rosie Phillips. While at Manassas—and, in fact eleven of his twelve years in public school were spent at Manassas—Larry represented the school on many occasions: in mathematics contests, Latin tests, and in quiz programs conducted by the daily newspaper.

In Larry's words: "My senior year at Manassas was one of the most memorable years in my life. It was a year of dreams

114

Larry Albert Jones

come true. I was valedictorian of my class and a recipient of a number of big scholarships."

Of the five colleges to which he applied he chose Wesleyan in Connecticut, where in addition to the National Achievement Scholarship he received the Pfeiffer Premedical Scholarship. During his three years at Wesleyan he was a member of the Biology Club; an active participant in the Black Student's Organization. As a tutor in the Middletown Tutorial Program for elementary and high school students in his major field, biology, he worked on a research project in microbiology and was awarded a Davenport Fellowship for summer study.

In June 1970, he was accepted to the Johns Hopkins University School of medicine. He entered there in September 1970, in the five-year Medical School Program for college sophomores and juniors. He represented Hopkins at the National Black Science Students Organization Conference in New York City.

Currently Larry is doing research under the department of pediatrics on cystic fibrosis, and in addition he is working on a couple of other studies. One of these is a retrospective study of patients seen at Johns Hopkins Hospital between 1964 and 1970 with cancer of the urinary bladder. This study is being done to determine the effectiveness of the treatment and for the correlation of factors such as age and sex in the rate of occurrence of the disease.

The other study is designed to obtain information for the development of a method to reduce patient waiting time in the office of a private physician in East Baltimore. For the last item he constructed a questionnaire and distributed it among the patients of this physician, to assess their feelings about the present situation and get some ideas as to what they think can be done to alleviate inconveniences in excess waiting time.

JAMES LEWIS FRANKLIN
Highway Engineer, Federal Highway Administration
Department of Transportation

A 1959 graduate of Manassas High School, James Lewis Franklin's major interest in mathematics led him to the field of engineering. He is now highway engineer with the Federal Highway Administration in the Department of Transportation, Indianapolis, Indiana.

Franklin entered Tennessee State University after graduation from high school, completed his training in Civil Engineering, and received his B.S. degree in August 1963.

He served in training position from July 1966 to May 1969, with assignments in the following cities: Eugene, Oregon, three months; Jefferson City, Missouri, seven months; Arlington, Virginia, five months; Washington, D.C., four months; Nashville, Tennessee, six months; Chicago, Illinois, five months; and Indianapolis, Indiana, four months.

He was signed to a permanent position in Indianapolis, Indiana in May 1969, where his primary responsibilities are to administer the federal-aid highway programs within an assigned geographic area of the state as delegated with immediate responsibility from the planning stage through acceptance of and final payment for federal-aid highway projects.

Previously he was employed with Washington State Highway Commission, Seattle, Washington, from May 1965 through July 1966, Bureau of Reclamation, Department of Interior.

He is affiliated with the National Society of Professional Engineers.

On October 15, 1964, he was married to Anne J. Holden. They are the proud parents of a daughter, Angela Marie, age six years, and a son James, Jr., two years old.

Dorothy L. Waller Pitts

MRS. DOROTHY LOUISE WALLER PITTS

Mrs. Dorothy Waller Pitts at present is Neighborhood Consultant of Social Planning, City Hall, Berkeley, California. Mrs. Pitts' accomplishments and participation in social and economic affairs have exceeded those of any ordinary person.

She was graduated at LeMoyne College, Memphis, Tennessee, in 1935, and received her M.A. degree at Howard University, Washington, D.C. in 1940. She has done further study at the following institutions: San Francisco State College; University of California School of Social Welfare (received certificate in social services from University of California). She also attended related conferences and courses at the University of California, University of California Extension, Berkeley, Stanford University, and San Francisco State College.

Her employment and experience since graduation at Manassas High School and LeMoyne College have been tremendous. She served as schoolteacher at Mississippi County Training School, Amoral Arkansas, for one year; librarian and substitute teacher, Manassas High School, Memphis, Tennessee, one year; teacher at Paine College, Augusta, Georgia, two years; worked in the United States Office of the Surgeon General, Washington, D.C., two years; staff assistant American National Red Cross in Phillippines and Japan, two years.

Since returning to the States her work has been on the West Coast. It began with her spending one summer as staff teacher, Summer Workshop in Education for Human Relations, San Francisco State College.

For one year she was resident director at DeFremary Recreation Center, Oakland Recreation Department; for the next eight years she was head director in residence, DeFremary Recreation Department; for the following six years she was supervisor of recreation, Oakland Recreation Department, and training consultant, Oakland Recreation Department Interagency Project. Her next move was to supervisor of New Careers, Richmond Community Development Demonstration Project, Contra Costa County Council of Community Services, Richmond, California. Meantime she served from January to June as executive director of Advance, the Negro Council for Community Improvement, Richmond, California.

Mrs. Pitts' membership and affiliations with professional and civic organizations are extensive: five different kinds of recreation organizations in the area in which she resided and the state of California. She holds membership in the church, the YWCA, Community Council, is a former member of the Women's Forum, former member of the Committee for African Students, former member and past president of the executive board of the Northern California Youth Council, Adult Section, and member of the National Council of Negro Business and Professional Women's Clubs, Inc.

Mrs. Pitts holds membership in Delta Sigma Theta Society, Inc., Chi Kappa Rho Sorority (Professional Women's Sorority); and others. She is the recipient of the following awards: Selected Woman of the Year for outstanding community service by Zeta Phi Beta Sorority; Citizenship Award for Alpha Phi Alpha Fraternity, Inc., outstanding contributions to Youth Award, Sunset District Community Council; California Park and Recreation Association Award for Exceptional achievement in the field of parks and recreation: Delta Woman of Achievement Award, Berkeley Alumnae Chapter, Biographee of "Who's Who of American Women—Marquis Fourth Edition 1966-67 Biography of *Who's Who in the West*, Marquis tenth edition, 1967-68, and *Who's Who* in California.

In 1966, Mrs. Pitts published a magazine article: "The Story of a Charm School." (Shows what good leadership can accomplish.)

Mrs. Pitts is married to Walter Lee Pitts. They have one daughter, who is married.

Presently Mrs. Pitts is sponsoring a Kenya student, who is attending the Contra Costa Junior College.

ROMMEL CHILDRESS

Rommell Childress was a premed student at Earlham, and as a result found no time for off-campus study. During his junior year he was named the most outstanding student in chemistry which earned for him a $200-scholarship. On merit and hard work, Tufts University Medical School in Boston accepted him with a scholarship to medical school where he is now in attendance. Although he has mentioned pediatrics as a specialty, he is not yet definitely decided.

MARY ROBINSON (Davis)

Mary graduated at Earlham in the class of 1970, with a major in elementary education. She spent six months in

Europe, three of which she was studying in Italy. She was married after graduation, and now is the mother of a young Davis. She is teaching in Richmond, Indiana, where she and her husband and baby live.

THEODORE JOHNSON

Among the many principals who are graduates of Manassas School is Theodore Johnson, now principal at Lester Elementary School and a highly respected administrator.

Samuel G. Eubanks, Jr. M.D.

DR. SAMUEL G. EUBANKS, JR.

Because of its possible human interest story which others have not bothered to tell, the autobiographical sketch of Samuel Eubanks is as follows:

My life was probably no different from many poor black ghetto youths, being a continuous struggle in a predominantly white society against seemingly overwhelming odds. It is very easy for me to see how a black individual can become discouraged.

I attended Klondike and Grant Elementary Schools from the first through the eighth grades. It was my intent during these formative years, to become a doctor. I don't know why this was my desire, or remember what my motivation was, or if there were a specific tangible motivation at all. But I do remember that this is what I said I wanted to do.

This idea was thwarted, however, upon entering high school at Manassas, at which time I became a band member and very interested in music. I must say that these, of all the periods of my life, were the happiest. I was so enthralled with blowing my trumpet and becoming a good musician that I had, during my four years of high school, completely forgotten all about medicine.

I worked through high school saving my money for college. My big ambition at this time was to attend Arkansas State and major in music as a cousin of mine had done.

At the end of high school I had saved about $1,000, and it took no genius to know that this was not enough to finance a college education. Being at this time the oldest of a family of ten siblings, I knew that if I were to go to college it would have to be primarily on my own. It was my decision to attend college, but were it not for two 'great' individuals always there to give me encouragement in difficult times, my mother and father, I probably would not have had the perseverance to go on.

One cannot imagine how just knowing that just two individuals like my father and mother are backing him, even if only in spirit, can give a person enough psychological lift to go another day.

I decided that I would stay in Memphis and go to college, and would hence have to give up music since LeMoyne College had no band. During my sophomore year I transferred to Memphis State University and experienced the worst period during my life so far. Attending Memphis State was much cheaper than LeMoyne, being only $165 per year for tuition, which I could easily work out and pay. I felt very unwelcome there, but knew I had just as much right there as anyone else. Because of the fact that when I started there physical education was waived and any extracurricular activity was 'off limits' for the twenty-one of us who began during that second year of integration. I have no feeling of compassion or closeness to the institution. I truly feel that a college experience is more than just going to school every morning to take certain courses, since a matured human being, who is to be fairly well rounded, is the alleged product.

The dean of the school of arts and sciences gave the twenty-one of us a talk before school started that September that I shall never forget. It went thus: 'We do not want you here. You are not welcome. We have fought this thing for many a year, and would like for you to know that the only reason that you are sitting out there today is that the Supreme Court said that we had to let you come.'

Things like having everyone that is seated in a classroom follow you to your seat with their eyes as you walk in, have an indelible psychological effect on any young individual eighteen or nineteen years old and, I think, inhibit learning to a great extent. I must admit that not everyone at Memphis State was against us, and some of the nicest individuals I have ever known were a few that I met while going there.

I graduated from college in August of 1963, and had financially depleted coffers. So I sought a job to work and save for medical school. I first got work at the Quaker Oats chemical plant in North Memphis, where I worked as a laborer for several months. A position later was available in the laboratory, where I worked the rest of the year as a laboratory technician.

I entered school at Meharry Medical College, Nashville, Tennessee, in September 1964. I spent the summer after my freshman year driving a city bus in Chicago. Also I was married to Hazel Shannon, an elementary schoolteacher in Memphis, at the time. She had finished Melrose High School and LeMoyne College. We had known each other since our early high school years, and had dated since our freshman year in undergraduate school.

She has made an excellent wife, mother, and a career woman since she is still teaching here in Flint. It takes a special kind of a girl to be a good wife for a medical student and doctor, and Hazel was endowed with the necessary attributes.

I finished Meharry in June 1968, and Hazel and I had our first child, a girl, on August 16, 1968. She was born at Hurley Hospital in Flint, Michigan, where I had taken internship. The time during the last three years has passed rapidly and I will finish my second year of a residency program in obstetrics and gynecology at Hurley in June 1972, at which time I will enter the Navy and serve my two-year obligation as a doctor and commissioned officer. I am on a special program (the Barry Program) which allows me to finish my residency but obligates me to a minimum of two years on its completion. I am now a lieutenant in the inactive Naval Reserve. After my completion of naval services I will go into private practice.

MR. AND MRS. CHARLIE COX

Both Mr. and Mrs. Charlie Cox of Gary, Indiana, are Manassas graduates. They have developed two fabulous businesses—the Cox Taft Street Drugstore of Gary, Indiana, and the Progress Pharmacy in East Chicago, Illinois. They are the parents of eight children.

Mrs. Cox and her family have spent much time traveling in the Carribean area and in Europe. She was voted one of the ten Best Dressed Women at the annual 1971 Easter Seal Luncheon at Vogel's Restaurant on March 20, and is active in numerous civic and social activities.

Mr. Cox has served nine years in the Pharmacists Association of Lake County and is the first and only Negro to be president of the group. He was elected for the years 1971 and 1972.

Gertrude G. Holley

Mrs. Gertrude Gaines Holley is the assistant director of nursing at the John Gaston Hospital, one of the units of the City of Memphis Hospitals. During the years of 1960-63 she was nursing supervisor at another unit of the City of Memphis Hospitals, E. H. Crump Memorial Hospital, and was assistant director of nursing in the same hospital from 1963 through 1970, at which time she was transferred to John Gaston.

Gertrude completed her college work at Hampton Institute, Hampton, Virginia with a B.S. degree in nursing education in 1952. She was married to Ervin M. Holley, and they have a daughter, Pamela Joyce Holley.

Her affiliations include membership in Chi Eta Phi Sorority, Inc., Harris Memorial C.M.E. Church, and the Mid-South Regional Medical Program.

MR. BENNIE MOORE, JR.
Director of Medical Records, Memphis

Mr. Moore was appointed director of medical records for the City of Memphis Hospitals in 1967. He now heads the record department for all three units of City of Memphis Hospitals, which include John Gaston, E. H. Crump, W. F. Bowld and Tobey Children's Hospitals as well as the Gailor Out-Patient Clinics.

Bennie Moore did the 1st through 12th grades in the Memphis City schools, and graduated at Manassas School in 1945. During his attendance there he was president of his junior and senior classes; was a member of the Ole-Timer's Club; The Speakers and Writers Club; and the Manassas *Newsette* Staff.

After graduation he entered LeMoyne College, where he maintained a place on the Dean's List for three years. He was a charter member of Phi Beta Sigma Fraternity, Beta Zeta Chapter, also president of the junior and senior class at LeMoyne College.

Mr. Moore became ill in the second semester of his senior year and spent several years in a hospital. After recovering from his illness he spent another brief period at LeMoyne College, and attended Henderson Business College.

In 1956 he was employed at the E. H. Crump Memorial Hospital as medical record librarian, attended seminars and workshops in medical records work in Boston, Massachusetts; Louisville, Kentucky; and Nashville, Tennessee. He was registered by the American Association of Medical Record Librarians in 1960, and served two consecutive terms as treasurer of the Tennessee Association of Medical Records Librarians. He was elected president of the Memphis Association of Medical Record librarians in 1968, after having served the previous year as vice-president. His wife's name is Kathleen.

THERON W. NORTHCROSS, D.D.S.

Dr. T. W. Northcross is a very successful dentist in the city of Memphis. He grew up in the North Memphis neighborhood, and attended Manassas School during his entire public-school career. He was graduated with honors. Dr. Northcross did his B.S. at Tennessee State University, and received his dental degree at Meharry Medical College in 1952. He did an internship at Medical Center, Jersey City, New Jersey.

His professional membership includes Shelby County Dental Society; Memphis Dental Society; Pan-Tennessee Dental Association; Tennessee State Dental Association, of which he is president; National Dental Association; American Dental Association; diplomat of the National Board of Dental Examiners.

His influence and help in the civic development of Memphis is highly felt. He is a life member of the NAACP; member of State Commission of Human Development; member of the Central Board of Boy's Clubs of Mephis; member and past president of the board of Goodwill Boy's Club; life member of Alpha Phi Alpha Fraternity; past president of Alpha Delta Lambda Chapter of Alpha Phi Alpha of Memphis; vice-president, Ninth District Democratic Club; and a member of St. James AME Church Trustee Board.

Dr. Northcross is married to the former Nell Patton. They have three children: Deborah A., who is in her second year in college at Mt. Holyoke; Theron, Jr., junior in high school; and Phillip Reggie, who is attending school in Memphis and is in the 7th grade.

DR. LEROY E. THOMPSON

Dr. Leroy E. Thompson is a product of the Memphis City School System, graduating at Manassas High School in 1947. He completed his undergraduate work at Tennessee State College at Nashville, Tennessee, with a major in biology. He

Leroy E. Thompson, M.D.

did his master's at Tennessee State University in 1958, with a major in zoology; entered Meharry Medical College in 1960, graduated in 1964, and interned at Hubbard Hospital in 1964-65. He did his residency at the same hospital in obstetrics and gynecology.

From 1952 to 1960 Leroy taught at Porter Junior High School in 8th- and 9th-grade science in Memphis. He taught at the University of Louisville Medical School, department of obstetrics and gynecology in 1969. After passing all his specialty boards in obstetrics and gynecology he had appointments at the Jewish Hospital, Methodist Hospital, and Red Cross Hospital, all of Louisville, Kentucky. He did postgraduate work in obstetrics and gynecology in Chicago Lying-In Hospital, the University of Chicago, October, 1970.

At present Dr. Thompson is director, Obstetrics and Gynecology and Family Planning, Park DuValle Neighborhood Health Center, Louisville.

His medical and professional memberships include Junior Fellow, American College of Obstetricians and Gynecologists; American Medical Association; National Medical Association; Jefferson County Medical Association; Kentucky Medical Association; Kentucky Obstetrical and Gynecological Society; Jefferson County Obstetrical and Gynecological Society; and Falls City Medical Society. He is a member of Kappa Alpha Psi Fraternity, and also a choir member and deacon, Third Christian Church. He is married to the former Ethel Isabel, and is the father of two sons and one daughter.

Beverly J. Williams, M.D.

DR. BEVERLY J. WILLIAMS

Graduated at Manassas High School at the top of a class of more than three hundred and fifty students, Dr. Williams, like her sister, Dr. Ethelyn Williams, was the winner of the coveted Sears Roebuck Scholarship. Beverly spent her entire school career in the Memphis School System.

At Manassas her extracurricular activities included the National Honor Society "Quiz 'Em On the Air" team; French Club, mathematics Honor Society (Mu Alpha Theta) and valedictorian of graduating class.

After high school graduation she entered Howard University, Washington, D.C., and graduated in June 1965 with a B.S. degree. At Howard, she participated in the following: Alpha Kappa Alpha Sorority; Beta Kappa (Scientific Honor Society); Sigma Phi Sigma (Physics Honor Society); Psychology Honor Society; German Club; Operation Crossroad. She spent two months in Tanganyika in the summer of 1969. She graduated from Howard University with high honors— *cum laude.*

She entered the University of Tennessee Medical School and graduated in 1969. She graduated with honors in psychiatry. While there, she was president of American Medical Women's Association. At present she is at Beth Israel Hospital, Boston, Massachusetts, doing her intern and residency in straight medicine. She has an endocrinology Fellowship at Massachusetts General Hospital, where she entered in July 1971.

RODERICK PETER DIGGS, JR.

Dr. Roderick P. Diggs, at this writing, is still a student but is no longer at Manassas High School. He is doing his internship, having completed his medical degree at the University of Tennessee Medical School in Memphis.

Roderick was an outstanding student at Manassas, and the prediction was that he would be the most likely to succeed in a class of more than four hundred candidates. While at Manassas he was an Honor Student aside from his participation in a long list of organizations and movements. Vice-president and president of Student Council; cadet commander of Manassas NDCC: citywide commander of NDCC, 1962-63; secretary of Ole-Timer's Club; National Honor Society reporter; Mu Alpha Theta (National Mathematics Organization) vice-president; member of football team 1961-62; president of Latin Club; member of Physics Club;

Roderick Peter Diggs, Jr., M.D.

129

Library Club; Future Teachers of America; Social Science Club, and made *Who's Who* among students in high schools of America 1962-63.

After graduation at Manassas he entered LeMoyne and pursued a premedical degree with distinction. From there he entered the University of Tennessee Medical School, and graduated in June 1971.

While at LeMoyne College, again he was a busy young man. He organized a volunteer band to entertain patients at Bolivar Mental Hospital; was president of Freshman Class, 1963-64; president of Sophomore Class, 1964-65; LeMoyne College Student Council president, 1965-66; LeMoyne Senior Class president, 1966-67; member of Alpha Phi Alpha Fraternity, 1966; LeMoyne College Dean's List, 1963-67; LeMoyne Christian Fellowship.

He was also on the Dean's List at the University of Tennessee Medical School, 1967-68; and listed in *Who's Who* in American Colleges and Universities.

Ethelyn J. Williams, M.D.

DR. ETHELYN JUANITA WILLIAMS
Graduated at Manassas High School in 1956,
and was that year's winner of the much-coveted
Sears-Roebuck Scholarship.

Ethelyn spent all her years from the 5th grade through the 12th grade in the Memphis City Schools. After completing her senior year at Manassas with highest honors, she entered Central State College, Wilberforce, Ohio, and earned her B.S. degree, *cum laude*, in medical technology. She then did her internship at St. Elizabeth Hospital in Dayton, Ohio. At the completion of this training, she was awarded the degree M.T. (ASCP).

Dr. Williams worked one year as medical technologist at St. Elizabeth Hospital and then moved to Chicago, Illinois, where she worked for another year and a half as a research assistant at the Presbyterian St. Luke Hospital. It was during this period that she decided to go to medical school, and was accepted at the University of Illinois College of Medicine. She was graduated from medical school in June 1967, and returned to Memphis for internship in the City of Memphis Hospitals . . . the first black female intern.

As her medical specialty she chose pediatrics, was accepted at the University of Oregon to do her residency; and in 1970 she completed her residency at the University of Oregon Medical School Hospital.

Pursuant to the successful completion of her residency she accepted work at the Tufts-Delta Health Center, Mound Bayou, Mississippi.

It is with a great deal of pride that she prepared herself to help in a disadvantaged community.

MRS. JOSEPHINE VALRIA JOHNSON-BRIDGES
First and only Black Public Relations Woman in Memphis.

Josephine Johnson, as she was known when she graduated at Manassas High School, is a most unusual person. After graduation from high school she attended Tennessee State University for her bachelor's degree, became a teacher in the Memphis City School System and remained in it for several years. Later she resigned to become a public relations person.

She is organizer and president of the Jo Bridges Positive Public Relations Organization; vice-president, Stripe Productions; member of National Association of Market Developers;

Josephine Valria Johnson-Bridges

member of Memphis Chamber of Commerce; Ad Club of Memphis, and Memphis Heart Association.

While in high school she founded the Double Ten Society; was Drum major of the Band; and voted the most popular girl in the class. Several years ago she was the cofounder of an organization which is now national in scope: JUGS (charity organization) which is made up of young women. She is also a member of Delta Sigma Sorority.

She is married to Anderson Bridges, a physical education teacher in the Memphis Public Schools. She is the mother of four girls—Veta Joe, now in attendance at Southern University; Kimberly Xunona, in the 11th grade at Hamilton High School; Keath Cheyenne, in the 9th grade at Corry Jr. High; and Kyle Virginia, in 7th grade at Corry Junior High.

HUGH C. ANDERSON
Listed in American Men of Science.

The following item was taken directly from the *American Men of Science*, a biographical directory edited by the Jaques Cattell Press, 11th ed.; the *Physical & Biological Sciences*, Supplement 5, R.R. Bowker Company, New York and London, 1969:

Anderson, Hugh Claude, b. Memphis, Tenn. May 31, 23; c.2. Organic & Polymer Chemistry, B.S. LeMoyne Col., Tenn, 47; M. S. Howard, 56; U.S. Naval Ord. Lab. fel. Polytech Inst. Brooklyn, 64-65, Res. asst. Org. synthesis, Howard 4-50, res. assoc. biophys, 49-51; phys. chemist, U.S. 52-64, res. chemist, 64-65; sr. chemist, Norton Res. Corp, 56-68; Prog. Dir. Polymer Res. 68—U.S.A. 43. Chem. Soc; Phys. Soc; Kinetics and mechanisms of pyrolsis of organic nitrates, pyrolsis of polymers and vicoelasticity of polymers. Address: Norton Research Corp., Cambridge, Mass. 02142.

Hugh C. Anderson

Rev. Wrennie Morgan, Sr.

'EV. WRENNIE MORGAN, Sr.

One of Manassas's most highly respected graduates in the ministry in Jenkintown, Pa., is Rev. Wrennie Morgan. He is co-pastor of the 3,100-member Emmanuel Baptist Church in Philadelphia, Pa. In Jenkintown, Pa., he is industrial relations director of the Opportunities Industrialization Center, and has held this position since October 1, 1965.

On his OIP job he analyzes reports of Job Development, Labor Relations, On-the-Job Training, and Technical Advisory Coordinator Committee to determine weaknesses and strengths of operations. He analyzes labor market trends in an effort to keep the training current with employer needs. He maintains contacts with middle- and upper-management personnel to smoothe the flow of information between agency and the business and industrial communities. In addition he serves as liaison man between all levels of management and this government agency, business, commerce, industry, and all units that make up the economic complex.

On former jobs he has been employment interviewer for the Commonwealth of Pennsylvania, Department of Labor and Industry, located at Hatboro, Pa., also agency director for the Cosmopolitan Protective Institute, has served as pastor of churches in Glassboro and Camden, New Jersey; and also serves as chaplain for the 9th District American Legion of Pennsylvania.

After graduation at Manassas High School he attended Roger Williams College, Memphis, Tennessee, where he received his A.B. degree. He did additional work at Temple University, Philadelphia, and received the degree of Bachelor of Sacred Theology (S.T.B.) and later his Master of Sacred Thelogy (S.T.M.)

Reverend Morgan is married to the former Miss Eugenia Johnson, and they are the proud parents of two children, Wrennie, Jr., and Sarah Louise. Sarah is currently a freshman student at Spelman College, Atlanta, Georgia.

REV. JACOB C. OGLESBY

"Somebody said it couldn't be done, but he with a chuckle replied, 'Well, maybe it can't. But I'll be one who won't say so until I've tried.' " This could have well been Jacob Oglesby when he came to Manassas School. He sold soap—six bars to the box at $1.25 a box. He had to sell a great deal of soap to pay $5.00 for his little room, his food, and other incidentals.

Rev. Jacob-C. Oglesby

135

Oglesby graduated at Manassas School in 1936 as valedictorian of a class of 160. For the next eight years he went through college at Lanke, Jackson, Tennessee, and Howard University at Washington, D.C., and the School of Religion at Howard—he worked his way through, finishing with high honors, and the M.A. and B.D. degrees, and all but completing his residential requirements for the Th.D. Degree, Boston University, School of Theology.

This well qualified young minister served as chaplain and instructor at Florida Normal and Industrial College, St. Augustine, Florida, and taught for two years at Lane College, his alma mater. He has been pastor for twenty-one years in Detroit, where he organized his present parish in November 1956. His church, Greater Christ Baptist, on Mack and Iroquois Streets, supports a Mission Station (Church and Junior High School, Liberia, West Africa) to the tune of $8,500 annually.

Reverend Oglesby served as board member of the following organizations: Detroit Council of Churches: Protestant Community Services; Gleiss Memorial Community Center; Baptist Training School; Committee for Better Schools in the City of Detroit, and former chairman of B. J. Rally for two years.

During his very active career he has done a number of other things, among which he taught Old Testament for ten years in the Baptist Training School; served as Assistant Secretary of the Wolverine State Baptist Convention; was supervisor of the adult Leaders' Division of the National Sunday School and B.T.U. Congress; is chairman of missions for the Michigan Progressive Baptist State Convention; was formerly president of the Baptist Minister's Conference of Detroit and vicinity; and is a frequent preacher at Religious Emphasis Week Services in Negro colleges and universities in the South.

He is married to the former Anne Harris, of Arkansas, a college schoolmate. Having no children of their own, they have been supporting nieces and nephews since 1951.

136

Currently they are supporting five Liberian college students in the States, and have adopted three boys, age nine—all of them, and a little girl age seven.

Reverend Oglesby and his wife, Anne, have traveled extensively round the world, and have pledged to continue bringing Liberian students to the States for their college education for the next ten or twelve years.

REV. HENRY LOGAN STARKS

This autobiography of Henry Logan Starks is unedited.

I was born in Memphis in 1921 and came from a family of four, father, mother, and brother. My brother's name is Oliver C. Starks, a graduate of the class of 1941 of Manassas. My memory of my father (Harry L. Starks) who was a baptist minister, is limited. He died in my ninth year. From the information I have been able to gather he possessed a fair education and was fairly successful in his calling. My mother (Mrs. Ella Green Starks) who passed away in my nineteenth year attended LeMoyne Normal Institute. During my father's life time she served as his pianist. She never remarried after his death. Prior to my father's death sickness visited our home and stayed for approximately two years. My father on the sick bed for a number of months and mother taking the bed upon his death for over a year. One might say that sickness never left our home but would take short vacations for mother was never well again—up for a few days and on the bed for a day. Sickness ate up what little cash and property my mother had. We were without an adequate income so my brother and I went to work delivering groceries, papers and drugs. We were the bread winners until her death.

She was a proud lady and made many sacrifices that we might continue in school. Upon graduation from high school I became identified with a company that operated bowling lanes. It had two lanes for Negroes and after serving as assistant manager at Wellington Street Lanes I became manager of the Beale Street lanes. I held this job until I went into the Armed Forces, two years and five months overseas. I was in the Medics and attained the rank of T 5. I was discharged honorably in October, 1946.

Rev. Henry Logan Starks

I entered LeMoyne College in January, 1946 and it was during my freshman year I became interested in religion. Upon graduation I became the recipient of a fellowship for study at the University of Chicago. I wasn't able to complete my work there due to illness. Upon my return home I gained employment as a monument salesman and it was while thus engaged that I felt the call to pastoral work and accepted a small charge in the African Methodist Episcopal Church in Huntington, Tennessee. Soon after my call to the ministry I went to work for the government where I worked for a number of years, later resigning to further prepare for my life's vocation at Fisk University, Nashville, Tennessee. Upon graduation (with M.A. Degree) I accepted part-time work as a chaplain at Western State Mental Hospital, Bolivar, Tennessee. I was the first black chaplain to serve this institution.

For the past eleven years, I have been serving as pastor of the St. James African Methodist Episcopal Church. Too, since my graduation from Fisk University I have earned the Master of Divinity Degree from Memphis Theological Seminary and honorary degrees from Monorovia College, Monorovia, Liberia—West Africa, and Jackson Seminary, Shorter College, Little Rock, Arkansas. At present I serve as professor in the history department of Memphis Theological Seminary being the only black member of the faculty.

I am married to the former Alma Lee Edwards, a member of the class of Manassas 1941. She holds a B.A. Degree from LeMoyne College and the M.A. Degree from Memphis State University. She is a teacher in the city school of Memphis. She is outstanding in her own right. She has received honors in her vocation and church. She was a delegate to the A.M.E. Quadrennial Missionary Convention, Los Angeles, California, July, 1971.

My wife and I have one daughter, Amella Yvonne Starks, who is a student at Saint Catherine Junior College at Springfield, Kentucky. She is a senior and honor student. She plans to complete her undergraduate work at Morris Brown College, Atlanta, Georgia.

I have served the community as: President of the AME ministers Alliance of Memphis; Chairman of the Financial campaign of the Northern Division of the Chickasaw Council; Boy Scouts of America; Vice President of Community On the March for Equality; and member of the Board of Directors of S.C.L.C.

I presently serve the community as: President of the Interdenominational Ministers Alliance of Memphis and Shelby County (a predominantly black group); Vice President of the Memphis Ministers Association (a predominantly white group); Chairman of the board of North Memphis Action Project a delegate agency of the C.A.P. with a budget of over a hundred thousand dollars in both cash and in-kind; Member of the Human Relations Commission of Memphis and Shelby County; Vice President of Memphis Inter-Faith Association, an Association of churches and Christians for the purpose of making religion relevant in the changing society of Memphis; President of the Down-Town Churches Association; Vice President of the Board of Trustees of Henderson Business College; Chairman of the Board of directors of Human Resources Development Institute, an organization dedicated to apprenticeship programs and expanding skilled construction jobs for blacks; Chairman of the Board of C.R.A.S.H., an organization sponsoring subsidy housing in Memphis; member of the restructuring committee of the Tennessee Council of Churches; and member of the Phi Beta Sigma Fraternity and a Mason.

MR. EMERSON ABLE, Jr.
Director-Band

MRS. BOBBIE B. JONES
Director of Music-Vocal

From the famous Jimmie Lunceford to Emerson Able, and from Mrs. Georgia P. Quinn to Mrs. Bobbie B. Jones, music at Manassas has been an invigorating and stimulating force in the lives of the students.

In the first place it is easy to say that the music teachers were not just people who heard them play instruments or sing songs. They were people who helped to look out for the interests of the students and helped to promote their positive aspects.

Emerson Able, Jr., himself a graduate of Manassas High School, and Bobbie Jones, have amassed thousands of dollars' worth of scholarships aid for their promising music students. Some of these scholarships are to many of the best music schools in the country.

Although it has been almost impossible to secure biographical sketches of many of the outstanding music products, listed here are some of the names of the most celebrated.

In opera is the well known Vera Little (shown next in this parade of outstanding graduates) and Alpha Brawner.

Emerson Able, Jr.

Bobbie B. Jones

Jimmie Lunceford

141

Others:

TERRY JOHNSON— Percussionist, Memphis Symphony, Symphonic Orchestra.

EDWARD TOWNSEND—In Pop.

The Famous ISAAC HAYES—Stax Record Studio, in Rock.

ELMER HARRISON—The Short-Cuts, Pepper.

FRANK STROIZER—M. J. T., Shelly Mann, Miles Davis, Basie Q. Jones, and Oliver Nelson.

CHARLES LLOYD—A biographical sketch is included.

GEORGE COLEMAN—Miles Davis, Slide Hampton, Elvin Jones.

HANK CRAWFORD—Ray Charles, now leader of his own group.

HAROLD MABERN—Freddie Hurbard, Miles Davis.

EDWARD LOUIS SMITH—Horace Silver, own Group.

JAMES HARBERT—Ray Charles.

GERALD WILSON— Arranger, composer, bandleader, West Coast.

HOWARD GRIMES—Drummer, Willie Mitchell.

HOWARD ALLEN—Studio strummer "Motown."

HARVEY HENDERSON—Bar-Kays.

JESSE BUTLER—Universal Sounds Studio.

HOWARD GREGORY—Lead Trumpet with Isaac Hayes—5th Movement.

WILLIE PETTIS, JR.— Guitarist with Isaac Hayes—5th Movement.

WILLIAM CHARLES HURD— International Jazz Band, Boston, Massachusetts.

HERBERT SMITH—Black Studies in Music, Washington University, St. Louis, Missouri.

JOSEPH GARDNER—Recorded with Horace Silver.

BILLIE HERRON—Thad Jones-Mel Lewis Orchestra.

CALVIN JONES—Musical Director, Howard Theater, Washington, D.C.

ALFRED BECKTON—Movie: Carmen Jones.

Vera Little

VERA LITTLE
Opera Singer of International Renown.

Vera Little has had a most exciting and successful musical career as a singer in the Berlin and Vienna Operas. She has gained the admiration of the most discriminating audiences of many citizens of Europe. Her dominating personality, and her perfect acting combined with the dark beauty of her voice often astonished both the public and the critics.

She was the first Negro to sing *Carmen* in Berlin. This was her first operatic role, and it was about this performance that the well known newspaper, *Frankfurter Allgemeiner*, has written. This debut was the beginning of a great theatrical career for this Negro girl. "It is a talent of a great class. It is a voice and musicianship out of ordinary," this newspaper contended.

When singing *Carmen* in Berlin, Vera was noticed by Maestro Vittorio Gui, who was impressed with her voice, and he invited her to sing before Pope John XXIII in Rome. This was a great success and made international publicity. She was the first Negro to sing before the pontiff.

Concerts followed in Milano, Florence, Turino; she sang all over Italy. Maestro Rossi was fascinated with her and invited her to Turino to sing *Carmen* in the Italian language. (Vera speaks fluent French, German, and Italian.)

One of her greatest successes was in Barcelona. It was said that she was one of the best mezzo-sopranos ever to pass through the house. This opened for her the gate to many opera houses, and in 1963 she was engaged as a regular member of the Berlin State Opera.

She sang Amneris in *Aida*, Ulrica in *Un Ballo en Maschera*, Guillietta in Hoffman's *Erzhalung*, Pretiosilla in *La Forza del Destino*, Baba in *Rake's Progress*, and many others. Her repertoire includes more than thirty operatic roles. It is as a member of the Berlin Opera that she has established her reputation as one of the best mezzos in Europe.

She gave many guest performances, including *Oedipus Rex* by Stravinsky, in Turino, and *Das lied von Erde* in the Scala of Milano. She sang Amneris, Ulrica, Guillietta, and many other beautiful roles in the Vienna Opera. For three years she was engaged as a guest, and since 1967 they have asked her to be a regular member of the house.

During her first year in Vienna she had the opportunity to sing in the Vienna Festival. She sang the mother of Derhne and, later on, the third woman in *The Magic Flute* by Mozart at the Salzburg Festival. Then came the recording of Daphne with Hilde Gueden and J. King. Two years later she sang *The Valkyrie* with Solti, from Covent Garden; with B. Nilson, with whom she had sung Amneris during her first year in

Vienna, she was her Aida.

Vera says that she often thinks back to Memphis, Tennessee, where she was born. As a child she had an exceptional voice. After graduation from Manassas High School, where she was discovered by the music instructor, Mrs. Georgia P. Quinn, Vera took her bachelor's degree at Talledega College and later went to Paris on a Fullbright Scholarship which she had won singing an aria from *Queen of Sheba* by Gounod. Before singing in opera she won a contest in Munich, and she sang more than seventy-five concerts all over Europe, including Portugal, Austria, France, Germany, Belgium, Scandinavia, Switzerland, and Holland.

Recently Vera was awarded the title of *Kammersangerin* (Chamber Singer) the highest distinction given to singers in European opera houses who have been singing for a considerable time.

In private life she is the wife of Prof. Dr. Styliancs Savvas Augustith. He is a known geologist-mineralogist, who is now professor in the Technical University of Athens and who has written a number of articles and books.

CHARLES LLOYD
A pride of MANASSAS' Music Majors

In today's contemporary music scene, Charles Lloyd is perhaps the best example of the trend away from categorization—toward the idea that music must be considered as a whole.

Lloyd, whose background includes everything from playing in Memphis at the age of ten with B. B. King and Bobby Blue Bland to a master's degree from the University of Southern California, is one of the first major musicians to contribute to the breaking-down of barriers.

He was, for instance, the first jazz musician to play either of the Fillmore Auditoriums (he did, in fact, play both—plus Chet Helms' Avalon in San Francisco). He was also the first jazz musician to be invited by the Soviet Union to play

Charles Lloyd

behind the Iron Curtain (previous visits by Americans were arranged by the State Department, which also did the choosing of emissaries). Obviously then, Charles Lloyd's interests and audiences do exist throughout all categories of music.

Born in Memphis, on March 15, 1938, Lloyd was exposed to the town's strong musical heritage as well as to the music department of Manassas High School. In addition to playing with all the local and famous touring "blues" bands, he was learning about pop from pianist Phineas Newborn. Later, while earning his graduate degree, Lloyd spent many of his evenings working with such West Coast jazz formulators as Harold Land, Eric Dolphy, and Buddy Collette. He taught school for a while, but finally decided to pursue his musicianship full time by joining the historic Chico Hamilton Quintet. After four years as Hamilton's "music director," Lloyd joined Cannonball Adderly and, a year later, he finally broke out on his own.

Since then, extraordinary reviews have come from critics in media around the world. From scholarly pieces in *Harper's* to personality sketches in *Playboy*, writers who inevitably have become loyal fans extol Lloyd's supreme sense of excitement.

Richard Saltonstall, Jr., writing in *Life*, said that "Charles Lloyd's creativity and high spirits seem unbounded . . . his compositions are rich and contemplative, reflecting his love for the classical impressionists . . . even when the music boils and churns like an angry sea, it all makes sense and is exciting to hear." Joseph Roddy, in *Look*, described him ". . . a towering man from Memphis, with more hair than a lion's mane and a way with a tenor saxophone that discourages virtuosos."

And perhaps the most frequent observation, from a recent review of a Reed College concert: "Charles Lloyd performs with total joy result."

In June 1970, Charles Lloyd entered into a relationship with Kapp Records. Lloyd's new album reflects his and the musicians' desire to expand their audience still further. Added to his usual arsenal of instruments can be found a Fender bass, electric guitar, electronic piano, ring modulators, and a theremin.

Furthermore, the repertoires have expanded to include pieces with lyrics written and sung by Lloyd. From "Moonman" . . . a comment on "today's world," to "Sweet Juvenia," . . . images from his past in Memphis, to "Hejira" . . . a flute suite inspired by the tale of the flight from Mecca.

Lloyd continues to uphold the quality noted in John Rockwell's recent Los Angeles *Times* review: "Lloyd has fused avant-garde jazz with rock, contemporary classical techniques, and nearly every traditional form of indigenuous American music."

Isaac Hayes

ISAAC HAYES
Soul Singer

Isaac Hayes' recent appearance in Memphis was written up in the *Commercial Appeal* on March 12, 1971:

Isaac Hayes, the soul-singing phenomenon booked for an upcoming appearance with the Memphis Symphony Orchestra, is featured in Mid-South, the *Commercial Appeal's* Sunday magazine.

The rise of the musician, from an orphaned boy in a

one-room shack at Covington, Tennessee, to his current mink-lined existence is traced by staff writer William Thomas in "Hot-Buttered Hayes."

The Memphis Symphony Orchestra presented Isaac in its Pops Concert on April 3. He was advertised as the first soul music specialist to grace one of their pops, which have earlier focused on varied types of nonclassical music, including country jazz, blues, Broadway shows, Viennese, and the current brand of popular music.

Isaac has an enormous following, as is evidenced by his box office. His rise to international prominence has been rapid. Until about two years ago he was known mostly in limited musical circles as a partner of David Porter in writing and producing songs for recording. Then he recorded an album in May 1969, named "Hot Buttered Soul," his first major one as singer, and its sales exceeded a million dollars. Then Hayes became a star.

"Hot Buttered Soul" came to be a popular label for Hayes' voice and manner, as well as the title of the album that propelled him to the top.

Isaac was born on a farm not far from Covington, Tennessee, was reared by his grandparents, who were sharecroppers, and moved to Memphis with them when he was seven.

In announcing plans for the Pops at the Coliseum, the Memphis Orchestral Society noted that the net proceeds of the concert would be split evenly between the Society and Hayes. He has expressed his intentions to donate his 50 percent to a fund to be held in escrow by a foundation until it can be put to use to build a home for the elderly.

During his high school years at Manassas, Hayes' music aggregation always shared in raising money for things such as band uniforms and other school necessities. Since his "mink-lined" rise in the profession, he has made large donations to his alma mater.

Barbara Duncan-Cody

BARBARA DUNCAN-CODY
Freshman Med student at the University of Tennessee

Since the acceptance of black students at the University of Tennessee, four black women have pursued medical degrees. *All four of them are graduates of Manassas High School.* The first was Earline Houston, then Ethelyn and Beverly Williams. All three completed their courses successfully. One is practicing medicine, and the other two are interning or doing residency.

Barbara Duncan-Cody, the fourth black woman to enter the University Medical School, is now a freshman. Mrs. Cody graduated at Knoxville College in 1968, married, spent two years teaching, and entered the medical school in the fall of 1970.

At Manassas, Barbara graduated in the upper 10 percent of a class of 380, and from Knoxville College with high honor. Her busy life at Manassas High School included membership in the choir, the Pep Squad, NDCC Sponsor, Mu Alpha Theta Mathematics Club, Honor Society, and Library Club. At Knoxville College she was on the Pep Squad, the college choir, Delta Sigma Theta Sorority, and on the Yearbook staff.

LINNIE REED

A very promising student, who graduated at the top of her class of more than 300, is now a sophomore at Pembroke College, Brown University campus.

At Manassas School, her activities were many. Aside from being valedictorian of her class, she was busy with many other chores. She spent much time tutoring students who had difficulty with biology or mathematics; was a member of the National Honor Society, the Varsity Scholarship Team, and a social club on the campus.

Linnie's major interest is to acquire a medical degree. She is taking all requirements for medicine as she pursues her college work.

She was the winner of many scholarships, among which was the Firestone Tire and Rubber Scholarship which carries with it fees amounting to $1,750 per year for four years.

Linnie Reed

THE GUY SISTERS

MRS. BEVERLY GUY-SHELTALL

Beverly

After graduation at Manassas, she entered Spelman College where she earned her B.A. degree in English; won the Wardell-Hughes Graduate Award to Wellesley (all expense for one year). She returned to Atlanta and received her M.A. at Atlanta University and worked three years at Alabama State University. She is now teaching in the English Department at Spelman College.

MRS. CARMELLA GUY-PHELPS

After graduation at Manassas she entered Hampton Institute and earned her B.S. degree in nurses training, and did an internship at Johns Hopkins in pediatrics. She is now a nurse at Holy Family Hospital in Atlanta, Georgia.

Camelia

Francine

FRANCINE GUY

Francine is a 1971 graduate at Wellesley College with a B.A. in economics. She has taken a job with the National Urban League in New York as research assistant.

152

MRS. LILLIAN PIERCE BENBOW

This biographical sketch was taken from Delta Sigma Theta national journal—*The Delta:*

Lillian P. Benbow was paid the highest tribute in Delta Sigma Theta by her sorors when they elected her the 15th national president during Delta's 31st National Convention held in Houston, Texas, August 1971.

Mrs. Benbow, who has served Delta for the past four years as first vice president, is assistant director for Housing Programs for the Michigan Civil Rights Commission. Her other Delta experiences include chairman of National and Standards Committee; member national projects Comm., chairman, National Convention Elections Committee; member National Convention Evaluations Committee, 1963-65, Regional Conference Evaluations Committee; president, Alpha Epsilon Chapter; president Detroit Alumnae Chapter.

A native of Vicksburg, Mississippi, Lillian Benbow holds a B.A. degree in social science from LeMoyne College, has done additional graduate work in philosophy at the University of Michigan, and done additional study in law at Detroit College of Law. Lillian was an honor graduate of Manassas High School of Memphis, Tennessee, where she won many honors including oratorical contests.

Lillian Pierce Benbow

She serves on the Housing Advisory Committee of the Southeast Michigan Council of Governments, Housing; the Michigan Interdepartmental Committee on Land and Water Resources; the Michigan League for Human Services; the National Association of Human Rights Workers, and the Task Force on Goals, Governors Special Commission on Michigan Land Use.

Among the numerous citations and awards she has received are the 1967 Alumnus of the Year Award, LeMoyne College, Memphis, Tennessee; 1970-71 Wayne County March of Dimes Service Award; 1968-69 Detroit YWCA Service Award; 1969-70 Metropolitan Detroit YWCA Outstanding Contribution Award; "Operation Understanding" Service Award.

Lillian Benbow is a talented writer and a much sought-after public speaker. She is married to Edward D. Benbow, drug coordinator for the Michigan State Board of Education. They are members of St. Theresa's parish.

ROBERT L. CURRIE
Federal Probation Officer
Memphis, Tennessee

Robert L. Currie is an example of another first since his graduation at Manassas School in 1956. He is the first Federal Parole Officer (black) in the state of Tennessee, and perhaps in the south.

In the following order he reached this goal: he enrolled in LeMoyne College, Memphis, after high school graduation and completed one and one-half years after which he did his military service. He then returned to LeMoyne and graduated in 1964. He began to work in real estate and in postal service. In 1967 he entered Memphis State University and graduated in 1969 with M.S. in Guidance. Meantime, he worked with the Community Action Agency during 1968 and was given work on the staff as counselor for 1970-71.

Robert L. Currie

Later in 1971 he was hired as the first black Federal Parole Officer.

Mr. Currie is married to the former Delores Flynn, whom he met at LeMoyne College. They are the proud parents of two boys and one girl—Anthony Currie, 7 years, Elizabeth Estelle Currie, 5 years and Jason Currie, 1 year old.

EPILOGUE

Manassas High School, the past fifty years, has afforded a great number of professional and other kinds of service people, whose record is not included in this narrative, many whose whereabouts were not known and others who did not respond.

In the health field, especially doctors, there are many whose names should be added, among whom are Dr. Dan Thomas of Seattle, Washington; Dr. Ray Anderson of San Francisco, California; Dr. Earline Houston of Philadelphia, Pennsylvania; Dr. Charles Smith of Hattiesburg, Mississippi; Dr. A. E. Horne and Dr. Clara Brawer of Memphis. This is also true of nurses, engineers, lawyers, and many other occupations not represented herein.

But as earlier mentioned, it is the aim to show that students have gone from this ghetto school to many successful and serviceable occupations. They have qualified for the "Ivy League" institutions, for the "Big Tens" and many of any other kind one could mention.

Today there are students studying at Yale (Zann Perry, Wiley Johnson, David Hollowell, and Raymond McDaniel); at Harvard (Rhynette Hurd and Dorothy M. Hollowell). At the University of Chicago are Catherine Branham, Charles Branham, and Nearer Swannigan; at Brown University are Sandra Hobson, Richard Grady, Robert Martin, and Linnie Reed. There are numbers of students at Elmhurst, Beloit, Vanderbilt, Wesleyan, Mt. Holyoke, and as far west as Grinnell. And Manassasites boast of the first black student from Memphis to graduate at Vassar—Phyllis Atwater.

156

PORTRAIT OF A GHETTO SCHOOL

This group represents some of the members of the class of 1955 assembled on the front steps of Manassas High School, Saturday, September 2, 1972, for a class reunion.

Members shown here are some of the most successful graduates of that year. They came from many remote cities such as Los Angeles, California; Washington, D.C.; New York City, N.Y.; Indianapolis, Ind.; Chicago, Illinois; Baltimore, Maryland, and other cities nearby Memphis.

Such occupations represented among them were lawyers, doctors, a trucking industry (worth more than a half-million dollars); fashion designing, teaching and clerical work.

Mr. Charles Owens, a high school teacher in Mississippi, was responsible for this reunion. He is shown on the end—extreme left.